Into the Street

A History of the
Brighton and Hove City Mission
1849-2009

Berni Bannier

Published by Brighton and Hove City Mission

Published by Brighton and Hove City Mission
Calvary Church Building, Stanley Road,
Brighton, East Sussex BN1 4NJ

2009

ISBN   978 - 0 - 9562410 - 0 - 9

Printed and bound by
CM Print. 61 Station Road, Portslade, Brighton BN41 1DF

Into the Streets and Lanes.

A History of the
Brighton and Hove City Mission.
1849-2009

FOREWORD

There is a perception, I think, in some evangelical circles that God only moves in power in nations far removed from the shores of sophisticated 21st. Century Britain. But no serious reader of Berni Bannier's account of the spiritual journey of the Brighton and Hove City Mission over its 160 year history can be left in any doubt that God has been at work in a powerful way even in this cosmopolitan city on the south coast of England.

Two decades have elapsed since the first ten chapters went into print in celebration of 140 years of the Mission "bringing the love of Christ to Brighton and Hove": the author was then General Secretary, but twenty years on continues his association with the work as a member of the Trustee body. And no less over its recent history than in its former years, the sovereign authority of God has been at work. Hudson Taylor (whose call to China came whilst seeking the Lord on the beach in Brighton) asserts that "God's work done in God's way never lacks God's supplies." These pages represent yet another testimony to that truth. Indeed, even when we may have got it slightly wrong, God's gracious hand has continued to provide!

The promise of scripture is "I will build my church, and the gates of hell will not prevail against it" - and at the forefront of that building process are those God has called to do the work of the evangelist. Some have been employed in a full or part-time capacity to further this ministry, others increasingly have come on board as volunteers. Some, like the apostle Paul, have planted. Others, like Apollos, have watered - but praise God that over 160 years He has unfailingly given the increase! Please pray with us that He will continue to do so as the next 160 years of the BHCM's history unfold - or until He comes.

I commend to you, therefore, both the narrative contained within these covers, and, above all, the Lord Jesus Christ, to whose saving grace it testifies.

John Prideaux (Chairman)

II.

PREFACE

In the early weeks of 1981, I was working at Ovingdean Hall School for the Partially Hearing when the name 'Brighton and Hove Town Mission' kept coming into my mind. When I got home, I found a telephone directory and looked up the number. In fear and trepidation I dialled. I need not have worried. I was greeted by the warm, encouraging voice of Rev. Fred Money who was to become a life long friend and mentor.

So began my association with the Mission which I served first as a missionary, then as Secretary and then, in recent years, as a Trustee. In 1989 I researched and wrote a history of the Town Mission to mark its 140th anniversary. Now twenty years later I have brought it up to date to celebrate 160 years. It has been fascinating to trace the social, political and economic changes which have formed the back cloth to the work of the Mission. In all the changing scenes of life the Gospel of Jesus Christ has remained the same, and sharing this message has provided the motivation for all those involved in the Mission.

There is a tremendous power in history that enables us not only to look back but also to look forward. In writing this history of the Brighton and Hove City Mission it is hoped that these two aims will be achieved.

First of all, we look back with gratitude to God for His faithfulness to this work. He has provided, sustained and inspired 160 years of service. In all things He deserves the glory.

We also look back with appreciation on all those lives which have been channels of God's blessing to our City. Jesus told a parable of the Great Supper. The master in the story told his servants to 'go into the streets and lanes' (Luke 14v21) and bring in the needy. A similar call has led men and women to become local missionaries. As well as the missionaries there have been thousands of local Christians who have worked, prayed and given money so that the Gospel could be made known throughout the area.

However, we look back in order to learn and go forward. As we read of the hundreds of children attending one Sunday School and conversions almost daily, we cry out with the prophet Habakkuk, 'O Lord, revive Thy work in the midst of the years.' We should not dwell in the past for its own sake but we should be stirred to want to see great things happen in our day and on into the future.

As you read this book I hope it will inform, encourage and bless you.

Berni Bannier. March 2009.

ACKNOWLEDGEMENTS

Many thanks to all those who contributed ideas and information for this book and who read through the manuscript. Thank you to David Hacker and Derek Brimley who provided a detailed history of their respective fathers.

Many thanks to Deborah Fleming for her illustrations.

Permission for West Pier illustration:-
'Reflections of a Bygone Age.' Keyworth. Nottingham

Photos of Brighton:-
'Step Back in Time.' 125 Queens Road, Brighton

BRIGHTON.

From the New Church at the Entrance of the Town.

From an Original Drawing by John Bruce.

Chapter One

Brighton in the 1840's

In 1837 Britain had a new monarch. Whilst still only 19 years of age the young Victoria was woken at 6 am to be told by the Lord Chamberlain that she was now Queen of Great Britain and of the Empire. On her shoulders was placed a responsibility and a burden that was to weigh heavier and heavier over the 64 years of her reign.

The inhabitants of Brighton must have wondered what difference her accession to the throne would make to the prosperity of the town. It had been partly through the controversial patronage of a former heir to the throne that Brighton was changed from an obscure fishing village into a growing town increasingly notorious as a centre for the antics of 'high society.'

Indeed, from the 1780's the Prince Regent, later to be George IV, chose Brighton to be his playground and so attracted a class of people for whom pleasure was the whole *raison d' etre* of life. Dancing, theatre-going and gambling were fashionable pastimes and pompous parading along the sea front became an important feature of social life.

The eccentric character of the Prince Regent found its ultimate expression in the building of the Royal Pavilion which began as a modest Marine Pavilion and became more elaborate as the years passed. This Indo-Chinese Palace became the Prince's sumptuous home whilst in Brighton and also epitomizes an affluent, self-indulgent life-style that was to contrast starkly with the poorer inhabitants for whom survival was the main daily task.

By the time the young Queen paid her first ever visit to the town on October 4th 1837, just four months after her accession, the population had increased six times from the modest 7,000 recorded in the 1801 census. Whilst she enjoyed some happy visits she became increasingly disillusioned with the claustrophobic social life. In February 1845 she decided to sever her links with the area. Soon the Royal Pavilion was stripped of its valuables and all furniture, carpets, porcelain and paintings were removed in 143 horse van loads to Buckingham Palace or Windsor Castle. In 1850 the whole Estate was sold to the Council for £53,000 amidst a storm of controversy.

Those who had anticipated a decline in the fortunes of the town need not have worried for in 1841 an event took place that was soon to more than compensate for the withdrawal of royal patronage. On the afternoon of September 21st almost the whole town gathered to witness the arrival of the first steam train from London. As the smoke billowed out of the Patcham tunnel and the engine with ten carriages came into sight, few of those watching could have imagined the impact that the 'iron road' would have on the future of the area. The Queen may have been growing disillusioned with Brighton but others were soon to discover its many advantages. Rich merchants and stockbrokers were realising that the journey time to London of 1 hour 45 minutes made it possible to enjoy the advantages of a seaside home whilst travelling to the capital each day on business.

Soon the ironically named Victoria Station was also to be thronging with less well-off passengers for whom cheap day excursions meant an escape from the smells and strains of the largest city in the world. Fares plummeted and by 1861 the number of annual visitors topped 250,000 with 132,000 coming to Brighton on Easter Monday alone. Brighton never looked back and the population grew rapidly as her reputation spread.

By 1849 the impact of the railway was such that Brighton was entering an era which was to surpass even the Regency days in its displays of wealth. However, the splendid carriages parading along the sea front, the gleaming white Regency crescents and the popular Theatre Royal were a whole world away from the life that was being lived in the overcrowded hovels nearby. Within a stone's throw of elegantly dressed theatre-goers were the homes of some of the poorest people in England. Engels referred to areas like these as 'separate territories assigned to poverty', where, 'removed from the sight of the happier classes, poverty may struggle along as it can'.

The guide book of the time says, 'Go to any of the streets off Church Street and you will see hideous old women, drunken old men, young men and mere boys hopelessly intoxicated, reeling and staggering in the road' . Charles Dickens who was at this time living in the Bedford Hotel where he was writing David Copperfield knew only too well about this twilight world of poverty and pain which he had observed in London and was to record so graphically in his novels.

Within the Town different religious groups were trying to have an impact on the needs around. Henry Michell Wagner was the Vicar of Brighton from 1824-1870 and together with his son, Arthur, was responsible for financing and planning the building of Brighton's largest Anglican churches. One of these was St Bartholomew's which being four feet higher than Westminster Abbey, towered above the slum dwellings which ran down to the London Road. Henry Wagner was very much a benevolent despot and a High Churchman of the old school. When William IV wanted the bells of St Peter's rung for him on a visit to Brighton, Rev Wagner told him they were only rung for the 'King of Kings'.

Arthur Wagner was influenced by the Tractarianism Movement during his days at Cambridge and combined a love for ritual with a missionary heart for the poor. It was Arthur who had initiated

*North Street from the junction of East Street
showing the Countess of Huntingdon Church
circa 1910*

and financed the building of St Bartholomew's. In Brighton he was keen to reach the fishermen who were welcomed to worship in his churches alongside the rich and famous.

At this time the Town was gifted with several famous preachers including the Rev F W Robertson who was incumbent of Holy Trinity, Ship Street. People came from London just to hear him, and Dickens described him as one of the greatest masters of elocution he had heard.

Another gifted preacher was the Rev Joseph Sortain who was minister of the Countess of Huntingdon's Chapel in North Street. His concern for those without Christ led him to be an important influence on the Town Mission in its early years. This Chapel had been built in the 1760's from money given by Lady

Huntingdon whose evangelical faith found its expression in planting chapels from which the Gospel could be proclaimed. In 1871 it was rebuilt as an attractive Gothic church with a graceful spire that dominated North Street until it was demolished in 1968.

As this was a time of revolutionary ideas and much political turmoil in Europe there were many who wanted to see rapid changes to British society. Even though the Chartist movement which wanted the vote for all men had been discredited it still had many supporters. Meanwhile in the Library of the British Museum a young man named Karl Marx was soon to be formulating a system which was to be even more far reaching in its impact on the world.

There was however another group of men for whom the answer to society's problems lay in a different direction. For them the Christian Gospel was 'the power of God unto salvation to all who believed'. This power could not only save from hell but also rescue men, women and children from the disease of sin which was ruining many lives. It was this ignorance of the Grace of Jesus Christ as revealed in the scriptures that zealous men wanted to end.

To the outsider it might have seemed that Brighton in 1849 was a place of Christian piety where the various places of worship were generally full on the Lord's Day but a closer look showed a large population untouched by the Gospel message. It was the needs of these unreached and unloved people that were to become the burden of some godly men who wanted a way to fight this deadly ignorance. By the end of 1849 Almighty God was revealing His plan.

Chapter Two

A Work Begins

One man who wanted to push back the tide of evil and ignorance was Mr Robert Bevan who was an influential banker in the town. Along with other Christian people he felt that the slums would disappear if they could deal with the sin that had helped to create them. They were distressed at the deplorable state of spiritual life which was highlighted when the Rev Joseph Sortain visited a dying man. When asked if he knew who Jesus Christ was, the man genuinely replied, 'Please Sir, can you tell me in what street he lives?'

Men like Mr Bevan were aware of the founding of the London City Mission in 1835 and a little later of its Auxiliary, the County Towns Mission. The object of these two societies was to bring the Gospel into the homes of the poor by sending missionaries to read and expound the Scriptures from house to house. As most of the churches in the area were failing to make any impact on the poorer classes perhaps the answer lay in this method of 'going into all the world and preaching the Gospel'.

During the Autumn of 1849 the discussions over some kind of 'mission' for Brighton were coming to a head. It was finally decided that a Town Mission should be established based on the same principles as those of the London City Mission. Men would be employed to go from door to door and they would be paid from funds raised by subscriptions from supporters.

All this required a properly thought out organisation so it was decided to ask for help from the Secretary of the County Towns Mission. This was a Sir Thomas Blomefield who probably came to discuss the issues at Mr Bevan's home at the beginning of December. At this meeting a constitution was drawn up and it was decided that the work locally should begin as an auxiliary of the County Towns Mission.

From the first the nature of the work was clearly laid down. It was to be undenominational. The aim was not to promote any particular church but to proclaim Christ. In fact over the next 140 years the Town Mission was to be the oldest Christian organisation in the area which continuously united the Anglican and Free Churches in a common work.

Another stipulation was that the missioners employed should be people of 'approved' character, and that the strictest scrutiny be observed in their selection. Their duties were defined as 'visiting from house to house, visiting the sick and dying, reading the scriptures, engaging in religious conversation and urging Sabbath breakers to keep the Lord's Day and to attend public worship'. They were to distribute the Scriptures and approved religious tracts and urge parents to send their children to Sunday Schools. They were to hold Bible studies and prayer meetings and adopt such other means as the Committee may think necessary.

The *Brighton Guardian* of January 23rd 1850 carried an announcement inviting all friends interested in Town Missions to a meeting at the Town Hall. This was to take place on Friday 25th January and the stated purpose was 'to establish a Town Mission for Brighton'. A small but enthusiastic number were present that day for the morning meeting. Mr Bevan was nominated Chairman. In his opening speech he told his audience that their object was 'to form a Town Mission in Brighton upon the principle of Lay agency'. He added that this work had been going on quietly for some time but now was the time for it to be properly established.

Mr Bevan went on to outline the duties of those employed and to emphasise that it would function in conjunction with the

'Metropolitan Town Mission'. Mr Bevan stressed the great need for such a work and emphasised that the new society would work with the local churches. He continued, 'When there was a cry that the churches were so full that people could not get in, then would be the time for more buildings instead of agents; but the present necessity was to get people to fill the churches'.

One of the objects of these first meetings was to invite public suggestions and criticism. Not everyone had a clear understanding of what was intended and there was opposition on two fronts. Firstly, some objected to the employment of laymen. They felt visiting was the work for ordained ministers only. It was pointed out in reply that the early disciples were not men with academic training but those who felt a call to preach the Gospel. It was also impossible for ministers and clergy who were already overworked to undertake even a fraction of the house to house visitation that was essential if the whole population was to be reached. Secondly, an objection was raised that for even the poorest Englishman, his home was his castle and so it was illegal and impertinent to enter his house. Although it was pointed out that the missionaries would only enter when invited, this objection persisted for many years.

Then the Rev W Du Pre, rose to move the motion for the formation of a society under the title of the ' Brighton Town Mission and Scripture Readers Society'. He too emphasised the need to reach people with the Gospel and to draw them not to a church but to Christ. His proposal was accepted and so the Town Mission was born.

The officers were then chosen who would act as a Committee and oversee the work. The first Honorary Treasurer to be elected was Thomas West and there were to be two Joint Secretaries, John Carr and Charles Eley. The Rev Sortain then asked that the meeting humbly record its conviction that in order for success to follow, the Holy . Spirit's influence was essential. Little did that first gathering know that over the next few years and on into a new century, God would honour their prayers and continually guide the work which had just begun.

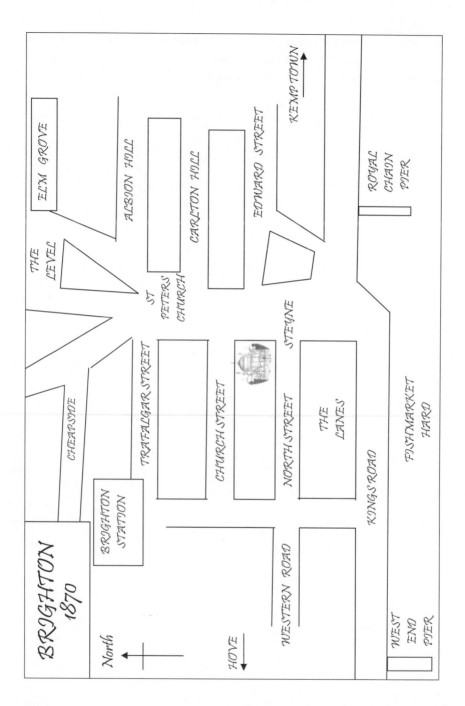

BRIGHTON 1870

North

HOVE

THE LEVEL

ELM GROVE

ALBION HILL

CHEAPSIDE

BRIGHTON STATION

TRAFALGAR STREET

ST PETERS CHURCH

CARLTON HILL

EDWARD STREET

KEMP TOWN

CHURCH STREET

STEYNE

NORTH STREET

THE LANES

ROYAL CHAIN PIER

WESTERN ROAD

KINGS ROAD

FISHMARKET HARD

WEST END PIER

Chapter Three

Early Days

The first missioners began to visit in the crowded streets and alleys around Church Street and Edward Street where few outsiders dared to venture. The work started with part-time missioners but it was soon realised that this was totally inadequate to meet the need. It became possible to employ full-time workers from 1851 as receipts for the first year were £382 and expenditure £180.

What these men found confirmed the worst fears of those visionaries who had established this mission to the poor. As they knocked on doors and visited damp, rat infested homes they found such poverty and deprivation that even the more socially aware in the town were to be appalled. Indeed the first year's report, written by Rev Sortain, was such an honest portrayal of the situation that one critic said it contained 'that which no mother would allow her daughter to peruse'.

Those first missionaries must have been devastated by the painful scenes of absolute poverty that met them. Families of nine or ten huddled together in one or two rooms for which an enormous rent was being paid. Indeed, a doctor visiting in Chesterfield Street counted 17 people asleep at one time in a small room. This room or rooms had to serve as kitchen, parlour and bedroom for the whole family. Added to this was the distress brought about by the winter weather, unemployment and illness.

One missioner gave a clear insight into life in his district, writing that 'there is not even the pretence of a bed, the family having only a heap of rags to rest on, and an old can in which to cook all they eat and drink. A few of the houses are inhabited by young women who live by sin and sin to live. The rest of the occupants are fish hawkers, watercress sellers or chair bottomers'. The reports are not exaggerated when they tell of painful scenes with adults sitting back to back to keep warm and children crying for bread.

Rev Sortain' s controversial report had been presented at the first anniversary meeting held on Tuesday 12th November 1850 at the Town Hall. It did much to stir the public conscience and over the years these reports were to have some influence as legislation was framed to remove the evils of bad housing and poor sanitation that was widespread in many towns and cities.

The report was mainly based on the observations of each missionary which they recorded in their journal. This was presented to their superintendent who met regularly with each man in order to discuss the work and pray. The Committee met each week and the missioners would take it in turns to appear before them and give an account of their activities as contained in the journal. For many years a precise record was also kept of the exact number of visits, tracts distributed, children sent to Sunday School and adults who had come to faith in Christ. During that first year 20,095 visits had been made, 22,434 tracts distributed and 92 people had been added to the Church.

One of the principles that had been adopted from the London City Mission was that of having each missionary assigned to a specific district. This meant that systematic visitation could take place and missioners could get to know the people in their district. One of the advantages of the terraced streets with their overcrowded dwellings was that there were always plenty of people around whom the missioners could befriend. During the summer months the locals would leave their front doors open or sit on their doorstep. The streets would also be the playground for large numbers of children who soon got to know and respect their local missionary.

Even with a total population of 60,000, districts were manageable and it was possible for a missionary to know the various shopkeepers, stall holders, cab-men, stable boys, as well as the residents. Areas in these early days included all the side streets off main thoroughfares such as London Road, West of Queens Road and off Southover Street. Those dedicated men employed by the Town Mission visited each house and if necessary, each room or lodging so that none would miss out on hearing the 'Good News' of salvation.

As well as visiting from house to house, the missioners also busied themselves in many other activities which ensured an audience for their important message. Open-air meetings were held throughout the year but especially during the summer months. These were usually near the beach on the Fishmarket Hard where fishermen would be washing their nets, or on The Level. It was not unusual however for meetings to be held on street corners and several sick people were converted on their beds as the voice of the preacher was 'overheard'.

Visits to Public Houses were also made and a vigorous temperance work started. Brighton was a town full of 'pubs' and beer shops. In 1860 there were 479 compared with only 111 bakers, and some streets had 20 or more such establishments in them. Drunkenness among the poor and in the slums was at an appalling level. Women and children were involved both directly and indirectly.

Visiting such places was dangerous but rewarding work. One missioner wrote in his Journal, 'One man threw some beer in my face and so the publican told me to leave. Some of the men however requested me to stay. One man said addressing the company, "It is no small thing for the gentleman to come here in this way to try to do us good, and then to have beer thrown in his face. I think we ought to listen to what he has to say." With the consent of the publican, and amidst perfect silence, I gave a

gospel address. When I had done several thanked me and one said, "I think you have done a little good here tonight".

In those early days a group of godly women also felt a need to be involved in the work of the Mission. These were times before the movement for the emancipation of women and it was practically unknown for women to serve directly on committees or be involved in public life. However, in 1854 a number of earnest and dedicated ladies formed a Ladies Association. They wanted to support the work through prayer and to raise funds.

14.

The leader in this movement was a Mrs Holcombe who called a meeting of all those interested at her home in East Cliff. They decided to work independently of the Committee but in harmony with it. Their main purpose was to establish a prayer fellowship on behalf of the Mission and to contribute money to maintain missioners. From this small beginning grew a work that was to play a significant role in the survival and success of the Mission in those first years.

So successful were the efforts of this group that in 1862 the name was changed to the 'Ladies Auxiliary' as this title reflected a much closer link with the Committee. During the last 40 years of the century they were enthused by a lady of enormous energy who gained support from individuals for the Mission. This was Miss Anne Padwick who from 1860 to her death in 1899 was faithful in her prayer for the work and through personal sacrifice was able to finance a missioner herself. She also started a special fund for a worker among the cabmen, flymen, goatmen, bathchairmen and boatmen who used to throng the Brighton sea front in those days. It was the vision, zeal and self sacrifice of Christians like Miss Padwick that over the years enabled the Town Mission to prosper and numerous lives to be changed.

Chapter Four

Battles Fought and Won

One significant feature of the last 40 years of the 19th Century was the absence of any major war. The long struggle with Napoleon had finished over a generation before and once the disaster in the Crimea ended in 1856 the government was anxious to avoid any large-scale confrontation. However, within Britain a war of a different kind was being fought. Poverty, ignorance and exploitation divided the land into what Benjamin Disraeli called 'Two Nations'. The local Town Mission in Brighton was to be on the front-line in the battle against these evils.

The Education Act of 1870 was to establish a system of state education for the first time. Before this, education was left to a mixture of private schools, National schools (which depended on local initiatives) and other church schools. In some areas large numbers of children had little or no formal teaching and so were largely illiterate. Parents were under no obligation to see that their offspring were educated.

The Sunday School movement which had been started by Robert Raikes did much to offer children an opportunity to learn to read as well as learn about the Bible. 'Ragged Schools' were, as the name suggests, schools for the poorer children, but the quality of education varied from area to area and from school to school. An educational census in Brighton in 1851 showed that although over 8,000 children were in some kind of school, there were still 6,500 children between the ages of 5 and 15 who did not attend school at all.

As the missionaries walked through their districts they realised that such ignorance was a handicap not only to knowing God through His Word but also to a fuller life for which man had been created. The Committee quickly saw the importance of schooling and in 1853 opened a Ragged School in George Street, Brighton. This was a properly organised day school for younger children with a fully trained teacher in charge.

In 1855 another school was opened in Dorset Street and then a few years later a third in New England Street. Through these schools hundreds of children were given a primary education and an opportunity to learn about God and His world. After 1870 these schools became unnecessary but for two decades the Town Mission had played an important part in the fight against ignorance and illiteracy.

Over the years reaching out to children and young people was to form a major part of the Missioners' work. Sunday Schools and Bible Classes brought many youngsters under the influence of the Gospel for the first time. The outstanding worker in this area was the missionary, John Bailey Haynes.

Mr Haynes had joined the Mission in 1851 at the age of 24 and remained a dynamic worker until his death in 1902. When he started visiting in his district he was often attacked or insulted by the local householders and publicans. He noticed large numbers of children idling about the streets and brought them into his own house where he taught them to read. This children's work became so large that new premises were soon needed and so a house was rented in New England Street. This developed into a Mission with Sunday Services and Bible Classes for adults.

Very soon this also became too small and a wealthy businessman, Henry Willett, generously gave the money for a new hall. This was the York Road Lecture Hall where John Bailey and his wife did a remarkable work. A reporter visited one Sunday and vividly described the scene. 'Last Sunday morning I paid a visit to one of those centres of Christian effort at York Road. At half-past nine a Sunday School commenced and nearly 200 children must have been present. With them were about sixteen young people who were the teachers. When this finished at 11 0' clock, morning worship began and about 80 or 90 adults were added to the children'.

The report continued, 'The service was strictly unsectarian. At a quarter past two the Sunday School was opened again and this time more than 200 children attended. At a quarter to four, some 70 or 80 young persons attended a Bible Class, their ages, judging from appearance, being about 20 years each. In the evening at half past six there was again a public service and the Hall was crowded. Mr Haynes feelingly complains that the room is not half large enough for the work that might be accomplished were there more space'.

This need for more space prompted Mr Haynes to begin penny subscriptions from the worshippers at York Road towards bigger premises. He achieved his goal when in 1881 the New England Road Mission became available.

Here all the old activities continued but on a larger scale. In addition to the normal services and mid-week groups, Mr Haynes began a tea for the poor and it is said that on average some 400 attended. He even found time to help recently released prisoners and assisted hundreds of Brightonians to emigrate

18.

to the colonies. All these activities were in addition to visiting from house to house and secretarial duties, all for a wage of £1 a week! When he died nearly 3,000 were at his funeral and included representatives from every sector of society.

The fight against ignorance which led to schools and Sunday Schools being established also resulted in another pioneering work by the Mission. In the 1850's books were very expensive with the result that even if the poorer classes learned to read there was little or no material available to them.

Even though a Public Library Act had come into force in 1850 nothing significant was done locally. So for nearly 20 years until the council established a public library in upper rooms at the Royal Pavilion the Town Mission collected quality books from supporters and lent them to the ordinary people. This Free Lending Library started with around 3,500 books and grew quickly until disbanded in 1870 once the council library was opened at Church Street in part of the Royal Stables built by the Prince of Wales.

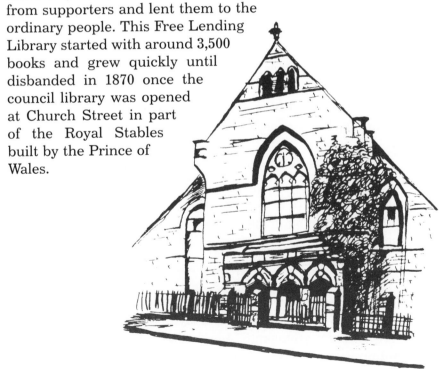

Another cause for concern for the missionaries was the appalling state of housing. Every day they were faced with damp, cramped alleys with little ventilation. Sewage, horse manure and household refuse were the breeding grounds for disease with cholera and typhoid common causes of death. Several Brighton courts had open cesspools in the centre which were often full to overflowing. The sewer running through Edward Street was actually higher than the basement floor of the surrounding houses.

The Journals were full of reports of missionaries despairing at the physical conditions under which people were living. One said 'It is scarcely possible that any good can be done in .... Street or the people can be better so long as the surroundings are so bad'. Some of the worst streets included Egremont Street, Little Oxford Street and Paradise Street!

These reports were cries from the heart and did not go unnoticed. Year after year during the 1860's, the Committee brought such conditions to the public attention. Some objected to this, saying it was not part of the work to be concerned about such issues.

The Mission however persisted in urging the authorities to bring about reforms. Eventually in 1875 Disraeli's government brought in legislation that was to have a beneficial effect on conditions throughout the country. By the 1890's some of the worst streets like Dorset Street and Nottingham Street were demolished altogether.

All these battles over education and sanitation were considered essential if the Gospel was to be truly presented and bear fruit. The evangelical statesman, Lord Shaftesbury, had said, 'We cannot hope to evangelise the masses unless there is a practical Christianity as well as a preached Christianity'.

The work of the Town Mission through its men 'on the ground' successfully combined a concern for the whole man; spirit, soul and body. However they never lost sight of the biggest battle of all which was over the souls of men, women and children. Over the years there were to be some wonderful testimonies of the grace of God bringing about changed hearts, changed attitudes and changed lives.

Chapter Five

Changed Lives

By the 1880's the work of the Town Mission was not only well established but also bearing fruit in the form of lives changed through personal encounters with Christ. The population of Brighton was fast approaching 100,000 and 12 missionaries laboured in this vast mission field.

The area to the West was also experiencing phenomenal growth. Hove had a population of 4,000 when the Mission was formed. However, by the turn of the century not only had it grown in number to 35,000 but had extended over the meadows and hay fields along Church Road and West of Sackville Road. As missioners had been working in Hove for a number of years, in 1886 the Committee agreed to a suggestion from Anne Padwick to alter the name to 'The Brighton and Hove Town Mission'.

Whilst some observers thought Brighton was shabby and undergoing a period of decline there were more than enough attractions to draw people. George Augustus Sala was a local resident at the end of the century who wrote about the Brighton he knew at this time. 'Between 3 and 5 pm, the Front through King's Road to Kemp Town and on the Marine Parade is crowded with barouches, landaus, broughams, mail-phaetons and dog-carts'. Sala goes on to write that, for the excursionist brought in by the railway, 'summer at Brighton means bathing; it means donkey-riding and driving in goat-chaises; it means much reading by young ladies of cheap novels, or knitting, or in some way whiling away the time in shady places or on the Pier.'

All this activity and pleasure seeking meant a small army of locals found employment, usually seasonal, as cabmen ferrying visitors in horse taxis, flymen, goatmen, bathchairmen and as stable hands. It was especially among these folk that the missioners began to see some remarkable changes.

One missionary wrote of his experiences among the flymen.
'As I passed a stand to-day a knot of the flymen were standing together and one of them said "Here comes our missionary". Then addressing me he said, "we do not receive such visits from others as we do from you and we are glad to hear you read the Bible to us, for by that we stand or fall". This man used to object strongly when I tried to talk to him but now he attends a place of worship, has family prayers, and sends his children to Sunday School. On another occasion while I was reading the scriptures to a flyman others came round me and asked questions. One man sitting on his fly observed, "This is what I read now", holding up his Testament'.

The missionaries' Journals are also full of encouraging responses as they went around the livery stables. 'One of the men at the mews met me with a hearty welcome and told me that a great change had occurred in Jim's life. Jim was a lad whom I had met one day grooming a horse and I had given him a leaflet. He told me that years ago he used to think about God but didn't care any more. We then read a few verses of the Word together which the Lord used to speak to him. I left, inviting Jim to the meeting that evening. He came and at the end said that the message had seemed just for him. From this time on he was glad to hear the Word'.

An important work was also being done amongst the railway workers. This was the hey-day of steam and vast numbers of employees were needed for the many different jobs involved. One porter met by a missionary was a sober and respectable family man but would have nothing to do with the things of God. Even when his eldest daughter died he refused all conversation on the subject. His wife, however, was a committed believer and faithfully prayed for him.

At length this railway worker had some problems and began to talk about them to the local missionary who had befriended him. During the times when they met together the wife prayed and eventually the railwayman gave his heart to the Lord. He began to attend church meetings and became so zealous that he soon got his married son to come as well. Eventually the whole family met together to worship on the Lord's Day.

As the Missionaries visited from house to house and from room to room it was often the women and children who they found to be suffering the greatest hardship. Often drink was a cause of the distress. Thankfully there were many stories that the missioners could tell of changed attitudes in husbands that led to changed homes.

One missioner visited the wife of an alcoholic who said, 'My husband loves drink and brings no money home. I have a large family with no rent for the landlord or bread for the children. It's enough to make me run away from him altogether'. The missioner encouraged her to look to the Lord for help and to pray. He told her of a man living nearby who had previously been just as bad as her husband. Miraculously this man had been changed and the whole family were now involved in the local church.

Whilst walking around their districts the missionaries would often be seeking the Lord quietly in prayer, looking for a God-given opening. Some interesting encounters resulted. 'I met a man coming down the street with a large dog. A more vicious man I never saw. I was led to approach him and told him that

God loved him. I shall never forget his look. He replied, "Loves me! No! No! I am sure He does not love me!" I showed him what God said about it. The man stood bewildered and asked if anyone had sent me to see him. I replied that God had sent me with this message of love and that none were too bad to come to Jesus. He shook me by the hand and said, "I thank you sir. You have saved me from doing a great crime to-day".'

Although converts were added to any local church that would nurture and care for the 'new babe in Christ', most found a spiritual home in one of the Mission Halls. These were independently run churches which were often established in the heart of crowded districts by missioners. They became a base from which outreach into the neighbouring area could be conducted and were a hive of activity throughout the week.

Most Missions catered for all the needs of the family with Sunday Schools, Ladies' Meetings, Men's Meetings, 'Band of Hope' groups and various temperance meetings. For the Christian family committed to their local Hall it was the focus of life. The highlight of the year would be the Church outing to the Downs on the Dyke railway or a trip along the coast to Rottingdean.

As the population grew, Mission Halls were built to meet the needs of these new districts. Money came through penny subscriptions or through the generosity of evangelical businessmen. Some of these buildings are still standing although sadly no longer serving their original function. The Bentham Road Hall was opened in 1883 and the Lower Market Street Mission in Hove was opened a year later. The Carlton Hill Mission soon became too small and was superseded by the Sussex Street Mission Hall established in 1878. All of them did a remarkable work in preaching a simple but powerful Gospel that did result in changed lives.

The Mission Halls were also the base for an important caring work in the community. In those days, long before Social Services and the development of the Welfare State, the Christians of the town played a vital role in meeting the physical needs of the people.

Through these Mission Halls, Hospital and Dispensary Tickets were distributed to the sick of the area. These were vouchers paid for by generous citizens who enabled the sick to have medical care which otherwise would have been denied them. During the Autumn and Winter, blankets were lent out on the deposit of a few pence which was repaid when the blanket was returned clean once the warmer weather came. One missioner records, 'No one can tell the moral and physical distress of the poor in my district during the severe weather. What they would have suffered without the Blanket Lending Society, the Soup Kitchen and one or two kind friends I dread to think'.

The greatest impact of these Mission Halls was on the lives of the children and young people. One of the superintendents at a Mission Hall recalled this remarkable story of an incident one Sunday morning in 1887. 'Knowing that several of the Sunday School teachers as well as myself were unwell I thought it best to try to get into the School to see how things were getting on. There was such a shortage of help that two classes were being taken by one teacher. On asking who was in the back room with the infants, I was told, "Only two boys as I have no one else to send".'

When I went into the room I found about 60 infants as quiet as could be, listening to a lad, Arthur, aged about 10. He was standing on a chair before them explaining a scripture card on the subject of Christ receiving little children. He was telling them how all had gone away like little wandering lambs but how Jesus the good shepherd was standing with open arms and tender voice asking them to come back to Him. Usually when

I go in the teacher stops but little Arthur went on talking to the infants. He kept their attention until the end of Sunday School which was over an hour. I am sure from what I heard that nothing better could have been said.'

As the century drew to a close, the Town Mission had been established for over 50 years. In that time a remarkable work had been done and undoubtedly Brighton and Hove were far better places because of this. No matter what lay ahead for the nation, the work of the Gospel would continue in the two towns. As long as there were Christian people with a heart for the lost and a desire to share their Saviour with others the work would go on.

Chapter Six

A New Century

The new century began with the aged Queen who had given her name to an era, still on the throne. However, the years ahead were to see changes which few could have imagined as Victoria's reign came to an end. As the crowds lined the streets of London in January 1901 for the Queen's funeral this was still a world without the jet engine, radio or television. The horse and the tram were still the main form of transport in the towns. However, new inventions and discoveries as well as new ideas were soon to transform society and influence the attitudes and life-style of the people.

Goat Boys and Flower Lady on the Hove Border
circa 1910

As a new century dawned on the South coast of England popular opinion seemed to consider Brighton rather shabby and unattractive. Even *The Daily Mail* ran a front page story condemning Brighton as an outdated holiday resort. Louis Melville writing of Brighton around that time called it 'a Cockney's paradise, the Mecca of the stockbroker and the chorus girl'. Like many other observers he was influenced by looking at a Pavilion which was so run down that it stood as an object of derision and a Steine which was surrounded by tramways and cheap boarding houses.

However, just as a Prince and a form of transport had helped to transform Brighton in the past, so now a new King and the increasing popularity of the motor car was to breathe new life into the town. King Edward VII enjoyed his visits to Brighton and these became more and more frequent. When it was reported in the national press that the King was enjoying floods of sunshine and fine sea air this was the best advert the town could have. As well as a new influx of notable people into the town, the excursion trade also profited from this publicity.

The motor-car was rapidly improving as a reliable means of transport. The speed, comfort and appearance of models was changing for the better all the time. Brighton proved to be a very convenient distance from London for those who wanted a 'run-out' and there were plenty of attractions on the coast once they arrived. The town had been chosen as the destination for the motorists who celebrated the end of the 'Red Flag Act' by driving from London to Brighton on 14th November 1896. This early connection with the motor car was strengthened when the Madeira Drive was given a proper tarmac surface in 1905 and various Speed Trials and races were held there.

It was against this background that the Fifty-first Annual Report of the Town Mission was produced. In it we read of the Committee's heartfelt gratitude to Almighty God for the blessings which have attended the work of the missionaries over the past year. However, it goes on to say that they greatly deplore the future curtailment of its work owing to the compulsory reduction of one missionary due to lack of funds. This concern over finances was not new as a shortfall in income had characterised many previous reports.

The root of the problem over raising support to employ missioners lay in the fact that few churches made contributions to the work. Only Emmanuel Church in Montpelier Place gave a significant amount. This was because the Rev J B Figgis was the minister and as a Committee member he had a great interest in the work. Only three other churches made any contribution at all. It appears that the work of Home Missions was not an attractive cause and it was far easier to raise funds to evangelise the masses in India and other parts of the Empire than to gain support for missionaries who visited those living on the doorsteps of the local church.

Most of the Town Mission's income came from interested individuals who would send in a subscription each year. Very often these were very small amounts of two shillings or less but these soon added up and were vital to the continuance of the work. Many Christians, some of whom were unemployed or widows, gave sacrificially because they knew the importance of the cause. At no time were any grants requested or received from the local council and indeed it was the 'widow's mite' given in love that God used over the years to finance His work.

The Ladies' Auxiliary continued to be an important means of raising support well into the second half of the new century. This was mainly through members who were appointed collectors. These ladies would collect subscriptions as well as spread news of the work. Up to a quarter of the needed income was provided in this way. Working parties to make items for sale were also organised by the ladies and profits from sales of work went into the Mission funds. In addition the Auxiliary collected gifts of Bibles, tracts and blankets together with dispensary and hospital letters.

After Miss Padwick's death in 1899 it was her nephew, Mr Gerald Padwick, who became the Treasurer and co-ordinated the work of the Auxiliary on behalf of the Committee. He continued this work until his death in 1949. As he had joined the Committee in 1893 he was the Mission's longest serving member. He must have witnessed many changes both in the local area and on the world scene during his 56 years in office. He was greatly helped by Mrs Townend who was Secretary from 1906 until her death in 1941. Apart from raising funds she gave considerable sums of money from her own resources in order to buy Bibles and tracts and to provide relief to the poor.

From 1899 a new venture helped to stimulate interest and forward the work. A Cabmen's Mission was started to meet the needs of the hundreds of men who earned a living waiting to ferry passengers to their stated destinations. A missioner was appointed who was especially interested in these men, their wives and families. In later years as horses were used less and less it became necessary to change the name to Cabmen and Taximen's Mission and a special work amongst taxi-drivers continued until as late as 1970.

In the early days of the Cabmen's Mission a room was rented at Cheapside where Sunday services and Bible classes were held. Here an extensive Sunday School work was done among cabmen's children and over 90 youngsters were attending classes on Wednesdays at 7 pm.

The Summer outings were eagerly anticipated and at Christmas large parties were held at the Presbyterian School room in North Road. The older folk enjoyed concerts of Christian music in the Cheapside premises and special suppers were also held. The venture was so successful that within a year of the room opening, the cabmen themselves paid the rent because they came to realise the value of the work being done amongst their families. The room was eventually given up during the First World War as most of the men went into the army.

For the parents a Slate Club was started. In the days before the Welfare State most organisations and especially Public Houses had a Slate Club where the workers could donate a small amount each week and then make a claim when illness prevented work. The Cabmen paid sixpence a week and during illness received ten shillings a week for eight weeks and then five shillings a week for a further eight weeks. In 1908 there were 70 cabmen using the scheme which encouraged thrift and responsible living as well as discouraging the men from going to the Public Houses for help.

Another way the Mission served these men was in establishing a coffee barrow. This was a smart, well equipped barrow which was moved around the town to the different stands where the men were waiting for customers. It was laden with hot coffee and good food at moderate prices which met a very real need and helped relationships to develop. Indeed there were many genuine conversions to Christ and one cabman reported how since he had given up working on a Sunday he now earned as much in six days as he previously earned in seven.

For the missionaries on their districts the day to day work was going on throughout these years in much the same way as it had done from the beginning. The men built up long term friendships with the locals by their friendliness and love. It was through serving people in the ordinary things of life that many of the working class came not only to respect the missionaries but, more importantly, to accept Christ for themselves.

'Need not creed' was the basic philosophy that guided the missioners as they helped in whatever way they could. Their journals are full accounts of jobs done whilst out visiting. Apart from the many cups of tea that were made for the elderly, there was shopping and cooking done for the housebound as well as wood chopped and coal fetched in. There were dripping taps to be mended, floors scrubbed and kettles repaired. Some illiterate folk needed letters written and even wills drawn up. All this was done to build bridges and without neglecting the main work of sharing Christ with the people.

Cases of distress were never far away as poverty and illness wrought havoc amongst the poorly clothed and poorly housed. In 1908 the Committee felt that some of the situations were so desperate that the general public should be made aware of the needs. They took the unprecedented step of publishing an appeal in the local paper on behalf of genuine cases of distress that the missioners had come across. As the funds at the disposal of the Committee were so limited and did not allow for such needs, a special distress fund was established. Major-General Finch agreed to be the Treasurer and donations were received from all sections of society.

Ultimately the overall response was disappointing and total contributions were small. At least the public had been made aware of the situation and the activities of the Mission became more widely known. Despite the limited success of the distress fund, some help was given to the poor. Food and groceries were bought and it was possible to provide for at least one needy family a day. Individuals were also donating coal and blankets to be distributed on the districts.

Since the formation of the Mission the Annual Meeting had been one important way in which the work of the Mission could be publicised. Year after year this was actually held in the Royal Pavilion. It must be remembered that this building was now owned by the council and no longer the sumptuous palace it had once been. It served as the public assembly rooms of the town and was used not only for civic receptions and balls but also for private entertainment, lectures and concerts.

The Town Mission held its meetings in the Pavilion for nearly 100 years until just after the Second World War. In the early days a reporter from a local paper would be present and a comprehensive report would appear in the *Brighton Gazette or Evening Argus*. It is a reflection of the importance of religion in society in those years and especially before 1900 that large sections of the daily or weekly paper was given over to re-printing sermons which had been delivered the previous Sunday.

Each year an Annual Report was printed and distributed to all supporters. These year books contained a summary of visitation done the previous year as well as news of appointments. It contained the balance sheet as well as a list of subscriptions received from individuals. There were details of the missionaries, their superintendents and their districts.

The most encouraging part of the Reports were always the stories of conversions that the missioners had witnessed. People were constantly coming to Christ and lives were being changed for the better.

One of the most interesting was when a visit was made to a dying woman. The account continues, 'In the little back room was a rickety chair, a broken-down bedstead and a piece of furniture that had once been a couch. On the bed were a few clothes instead of blankets which had gone to the pawnshop. The husband, a surly fellow, answered the door. The black look on his face plainly showed that he resented my intrusion. After a few cheery words and a few texts of scripture, he closed the door in my face. I walked away disappointed and feeling such a failure.

A few days afterwards a note was pushed through my letter-box from this same man asking me to call again. When I returned I was immediately taken into the room where the poor woman was lying. She was paralysed and didn't have long to live. Her breath came in short gasps and she could only speak with difficulty. She stammered that she had heard me quoting scripture to her husband and had sent for me because she wanted to know something of Jesus. I told her the simple Gospel story. With tears streaming down her face, which glistened as they trembled for a moment on her cheek bones, she gave her heart to Him who had given His life for her.'

Over the troubled years that lay ahead this wonderful love would continue meeting people in their hour of need. Whether it was through a tract read in the trenches of Flanders or a message heard in the back streets of Brighton, the concern of all those connected with the Town Mission was that everyone should have an opportunity to know the One who came to heal the broken-hearted and set the captive free.

Chapter Seven

A Time for War

August 3rd 1914 was Bank Holiday Monday and Brighton was bursting at the seams. Concerns about travelling to the Continent, together with beautiful weather in the middle of a glorious summer meant even more visitors than usual. Even the rumours of war encouraged people to enjoy themselves while they could. The excursion trains from London were so crowded that people stood all the way in the guard's van. Volk's Railway, the tramways and the deck-chair men all did a roaring trade. Whilst Europe teetered on the brink of a devastating war, Britain it seems, had resolved to 'keep on smiling'.

The war did come. The day after that famous Bank Holiday, the official announcement was made. Over the months and through four long years, the war became all too real. Jingoistic fervour would give way to grief and sadness. The young men who were meant to be 'home by Christmas' would be caught up in a struggle so horrific that few could have even imagined it. Millions would die before the slaughter ended in 1918.

The outbreak of war presented the missionaries with new opportunities to spread the Gospel. Brighton was used as a staging post for soldiers on their way to the front-line and so thousands of men passed through the town. The military authorities gave permission for visits to be made to the troops and the missionaries were keen to help in whatever way they could.

A special feature of the work was the distribution of huge amounts of Bibles, New Testaments and scripture portions to the men. The response seems to have been excellent and there was an eagerness to receive these gifts which was rarely if ever seen in peace time. Obviously, men facing death were looking to the Word of God for comfort and encouragement. Many soldiers were led to Christ by the missionaries. These new converts then took or sent literature to their comrades in the trenches.

The Bibles were generously supplied by the Scripture Gift Mission or the Trinitarian Bible Society. Friends of the Mission also contributed considerable sums for buying literature and especially the thousands of tracts that were distributed. Exact figures are not available but it is known that 22,732 pieces of literature were given out during the first five months of the war.

In September 1914 the first batch of 300 wounded soldiers arrived in Brighton and were taken to the 2nd Eastern General Hospital at the Grammar School building in Dyke Road. The terrible wounds inflicted by modern shells shocked the locals out of their complacency. The fact that these soldiers were no more than boys added to the sense of shock. Over the years the sight of the telegraph boy became a dreaded figure as more and more sons and fathers died in the Flanders mud. The missionaries found a wonderful openness to the things of God during these unhappy years and were seen by the authorities as important counsellors who were well known to the locals and were real friends in a time of need.

This friendship also took the form of making the soldiers feel 'at home' during their time in Brighton. As well as taking men to their own homes, the missioners also introduced them to Christian families. Life-long friendships must have resulted from this hospitality and many became committed Christians because of this.

The missioners also spent many hours in visiting the wounded in hospital. Even as they set out each day they would have heard the rumble of guns that made the people along the South coast aware of the battles that were being fought just across the Channel. One place they would have visited was the Royal Pavilion because at the suggestion of King George V it had been converted into a hospital for wounded Indian soldiers. The soldiers came from various castes and religions and we can only guess if any came to Christ during their time in Brighton.

It was ironic that, for the rich at least, 1917 was a year of 'phenomenal prosperity'. Some entertainments were re-opened and there was an influx of influential visitors and refugees. Some were escaping from the turmoil in Russia and others were the less welcome munitions profiteers whose presence angered many of the poorer inhabitants of the town.

Indeed, for the poor, times were exceptionally hard and the divisions in society especially obvious. The lack of food in the shops and the unfair distribution of supplies led eventually to a massive march in January 1918 to the offices of the Brighton Food Committee. As a result some minor changes were made but the poor still struggled to survive.

All the time the missionaries went faithfully about their work bringing comfort and help where they could and sharing their faith. One lady recollects how as a small girl of three or four she first met one of the missioners. 'One day my mother took me to visit an aged aunt in Elm Grove. Whilst we were there a missioner arrived from the Town Mission. I thought how kind he was to visit and talk to my aunt. Then he opened his Bible and read to her. As he prayed I remember thinking that this gentleman must really love Jesus'. The kindness and care of the missionary so impressed that little girl all those years ago that she still supports the work and takes an interest in all that is done.

Finally, in November 1918 it was all over. Celebrations in Brighton were rather muted as people remembered the horrors of the previous four years. For the Mission the work had to go on especially as the population is estimated to have increased by 30,000 during the war. A peace treaty was signed at Versailles but the next 20 years were to prove that it was a very shallow peace. On the international scene wars and rumours of wars were to fill many headlines and in Britain the 'land fit for heroes' which Lloyd-George had promised became an impossible dream for many.

Soldiers returning from the war found many changes, not least in their domestic lives. Their babies had grown into unrecognisable children and their wives had had a taste of working life in canteens and factories. It was as difficult for the wives as for their demobbed husbands to settle back into the old routines with comparative strangers. Consumer goods like clothes and furniture were scarce and rationing still restricted food supplies. In 1919 an influenza bug swept through Europe. It killed 150,000 people in England and Wales during the winter which was a hundred times the civilian casualty figures from enemy action during the war.

Even Brighton and Hove during the early 1920' s took time to recover from the depressive reaction that set in after the war. Poverty and despair were still the way of life for thousands of Brightonians in their cramped houses in the Carlton Hill area and off Edward Street. Violence was never far away and the town got a reputation as a place of vicious gangs who centred their activities upon the race course. Policemen patrolled some areas only in pairs and several horrific murders led to Brighton being dubbed 'The Queen of Slaughtering Places'.

But recover it did. The Town Mission Report for 1929 noted that opportunities were growing as the towns enlarged their boundaries. There were new districts to be covered as slum areas were being cleared and new estates were springing up on the outskirts. Only six missionaries were employed for a total population that had grown to over 200,000 and for an area that had increased in size from 2,714 acres to 12,565 acres the previous year.

Carlton Row Slums 1930

The main reason for this huge growth in area was the foresight of one councillor. This was Herbert Carden who became known as the 'Father of Modern Brighton' after his death in 1941. He acquired for the Borough vast areas of Downland that included parts of the parishes of Patcham, West Blatchington and Falmer as well as Rottingdean and Ovingdean. He realised the need to encircle Brighton with a green belt of downland to safeguard it from development and to preserve the water supply.

Herbert Carden also wanted to see the ordinary person properly housed. During his time in office the Carlton Hill area was cleared of its slums and new 'garden estates' were built to the North and East of the town. The main estates had nearly 3,000 new homes and were sited at Moulsecoomb, Whitehawk and Manor Farm. The quality of these houses were far superior to those being built privately and town planners were coming from all over the country to study their layout. Those who were re-housed were amazed to find themselves in a three-bedroomed house which had a garden as well as an inside toilet and bathroom.

With the two towns undergoing rapid changes in the inter-war period the Committee had to keep up with the times. In 1933 it was decided to include the Whitehawk estate as a new district and so Arthur Hughes who had worked with the London City Mission was appointed.

Meanwhile growth in West Hove, especially to the North of the railway line, meant that the area needed to be divided into two and the work was shared between Sammy Millar and Mr Hacker. As taxis had largely ousted the old-fashioned cab driver, the name of this work was changed to 'Missionary to Cabmen and Taximen'. Mr Ernest Waldron did this specialist work for many years which included befriending the goat-boys and bathchairmen which were still a feature of life along the sea front.

In September 1939 the uneasy peace was finally broken and it was once again a time for war. Brighton was soon crowded with children who had been evacuated from London. Around 30,000 arrived in the area in September and this created tremendous problems for those who had opened their homes. Many of these youngsters were from the London slums and they found themselves in a strange environment separated from their parents. As schools were shared with the newcomers it meant that the children went for only half of the day and so had plenty of time on their hands.

The Town Missionaries immediately set up meetings in church halls where the children could come. They gave lantern talks on all kinds of interesting topics as well as Bible stories. Every Tuesday afternoon at Islingword Road Mission Hall over 400 children were catered for with talks and lantern shows. Some of the teachers who came with the children from London spoke very highly of this work.

For the seven missionaries employed during the years of the Second World War there were many new challenges as well as opportunities. Their importance was recognised in the fact that among one of the few reserved occupations retained by the Government was that of lay evangelist which included those missioners of military age.

During 1940 the war came right to the doorstep of the twin towns. In June many local craft were used to evacuate troops from the beaches of Northern France in what was truly a deliverance of God. The 'miracle of Dunkirk' was a great answer to prayer and the nation was so grateful that Sunday 9th June was appointed as a Day of National Thanksgiving.

In July enemy bombs fell on Kemp Town and the work of the missionaries took on a new dimension. There was no single heavy attack on Brighton but hit and run raiders throughout the war left over 200 dead and over 1,000 homes destroyed or seriously damaged. A raid using high explosive bombs hit a cinema in Kemp Town where children were watching a Saturday matinee. The local missionary, Dan Brimley, and the members of the Pelham Mission distributed clothes, blankets, beds and mattresses to those left homeless as well as comforting the bereaved.

Opportunities to serve the local community were many and there were also new openings for the Word of God. Homes in one particular street were closed to the missioner as he tried to befriend the people. However, when Morrison shelters were issued in this street, he undertook to erect the shelters with help from some of the young people in the Church. His offer was quickly accepted and new friendships were made. One lad reported back, 'Shelter up all right, Sir, and I've invited them all to the mission hall on Sunday'. Many homes in that street opened up for regular prayer meetings and Bible study because of the help given.

One of the worst moments of the war for the country was the disastrous Dieppe raid. The landing on the French coast in 1942 resulted in many deaths and injuries and some of the wounded were treated in Brighton.

A missionary met four badly wounded soldiers on the Sunday after the raid. They were especially open to talking about eternal issues. A small service was held during which the sirens sounded and it was difficult to be heard. The chorus 'Wounded for Me' was sung and as the missioner thanked the sailors for being wounded for him, he explained how Christ had been wounded for them. The message struck home and a deep impression was made on the sailors who eagerly received Gospels.

On May 8th 1945 the church bells rang out for the first time since the outbreak of war, to celebrate a long awaited victory. A time of war was to give way to a time of peace. The particular problems and challenges which the war brought were now over. As the Town Mission looked towards its centenary, the work of visiting from house to house would continue as the missionaries sought to share their message of a peace that lasts with a world that had known only years of war and strife.

Chapter Eight

Men of Character

One of the foundation principles of the Town Mission was to employ men of 'approved character' and qualifications to give themselves entirely to the work of evangelism. Over the years the Mission and indeed the twin towns were blessed with a succession of men (and women) who not only loved their Lord but who were able to share their experience of God with others.

They were exceptional people not because they were necessarily more gifted or zealous than others but because they went out humbly trusting God to work through them. Each one needed to be a person of faith who knew that God was sufficient to help them through every situation.

They went out into a world that often rejected them and their message just as it had rejected and crucified the Saviour whom they served. In the early years they came into daily contact with diseases that were infectious and dangerous. They went into homes where no-one else would dare to go. They were always confronting suffering, sin and death. They were often people 'of whom the world was not worthy'.

Each missionary employed has a story to tell, firstly, of God's working in their own life and, secondly, of how they were called into His service. Of the scores of workers who came on to the Mission staff we can only look at two or three lives in more detail. We will look in particular at one man who in many ways was a typical missionary and whose life and witness is an excellent example of how the Lord can work through those fully committed to Him.

Daniel Brimley was born in the Lanes in the heart of Brighton in 1888. He was the youngest child in a family of seven but four of his brothers and sisters died of tuberculosis before reaching their teens. His father died when Dan was three, leaving his mother to bring up the family. She was an invalid who was greatly helped through the difficult years by her strong Christian faith.

Whilst still only three, Dan had to help his brother John (aged five) to provide for the family. They used to get up at 4 am and meet the newspaper train at Brighton station. They pulled their hand cart loaded with papers around to local newsagents and this took most of the morning. The money they earned meant that their mother could give the family one good meal a day but it also meant that Dan could only attend school during the afternoon.

Daniel grew up amongst the tiny terraced houses of the Lanes and soon ignored the Christian example of his mother. He linked up with a gang of youths who used to roam the streets and spent their time smoking and drinking in their 'den' which was a loft above one of the stables in the Lanes.

When he was 18 he was going past the Glynn Vivian Miners' Mission in Union Street (this became the Elim Church from 1927-1988). His gang were verbally abusing the steward on the door who was inviting people in to hear the preaching of a converted hangman. This man was a registered government hangman who had carried out many executions until he had become a Christian.

The gang, with Dan leading them, decided to go into the meeting for a laugh. During the sermon which began with details of how public executions were performed, the preacher then pointed to the One who had died on the cross to save us from a fate far worse than hanging. At the appeal, Daniel and at least half of the gang went forward and committed their lives to Christ.

That memorable evening was December 9th 1906. In the weeks that followed all the gang came to Christ and their den became a place of prayer and Bible study. They went out into the Lanes to witness and share their faith. Their early enthusiasm for the Gospel was noticed by Frank Penfold who was well known in those days for the tent crusades he conducted all over the country. He invited Dan to join the team on a crusade to miners in Northumberland. Although he was now the bread winner for the family, his mother advised him to go, knowing that the Lord would provide.

Dan and about half of the gang went up North and helped to erect the tents as well as preach and lead the services. Frank Penfold would stand outside the tent to see if he could hear the speakers clearly. On the first night, Mr Penfold remonstrated with Dan, telling him he could not be heard. He recommended that Dan spend the night on a nearby hill, shouting at the top of his voice until it became stronger.

The next night Dan's voice was like a fog horn. 'So you took my advice then', said Frank Penfold. 'I did not!', came Dan's reply. 'I went back to my digs and got on my knees and told God that if He wanted me in this work He would have to give me the voice I needed'. That voice stayed with him until his dying day and was much used in open air preaching.

After a year away from Brighton, Dan returned home. He began work with the contractors, Field and Cox, and attended the Pelham Mission in Upper Bedford Street. In 1932 he had a serious heart attack and was confined to bed for 18 months. During that time God was speaking to him and he promised that if his life was spared he would serve God in full time work for the rest of his life. From that moment he made a remarkable recovery and the next day he was able to stand for the first time in a year and a half.

He applied to the Brighton and Hove Town Mission. However, the President in those days was a Harley Street physician and on seeing Dan's medical record he said that the Mission could not employ him but he could work as a volunteer. Dan's wife, Daisy, took in lodgers to support them whilst Dan worked unpaid for the Town Mission. After three months he was called before the Committee and told that as his recovery seemed complete and God was obviously blessing his door to door work they would now be able to employ him full time.

He became well known, especially in Kemp Town where his outgoing personality won him many friends. He was affectionately known in the town as 'Happy Dan' and always wore a bow tie. Like all missionaries he seemed to be on call 24 hours a day. During the middle of the night his door bell would often be rung by someone who needed the signature of a minister of religion in order to get free treatment from a doctor. Dan would then accompany them to the hospital and help the family in whatever way he could.

During the Second World War he was a 'Fire Watcher' and also responsible for evacuating children from St Luke's School if there was an invasion. He was a man with a tremendous faith in his God. On one occasion the police called him to a house in Tillstone Street

(Standing left to right)
Mr H.Hacker Mr S.Millar
Mr Russell Mr S.Warner
Mr D.Brimley
(Seated) Mrs Hacker Mrs Russell
Mrs Warner Mrs Brimley

where there were two ladies. One of them had become senile and violent and was holding a carving knife to her companion's throat. The police and doctor were unable to do anything, so they called Dan. He arrived at the house and had a word of prayer at the door. Then he calmly walked in and took the knife from the old lady's hand.

Dan Brimley is a wonderful example of how God can use any life fully committed to Him. It is remarkable to think how a man from such a poor background and with so little education was used by God and became an eloquent preacher, a practical man and a friend to all with whom he came into contact.

Another outstanding missionary of that time was Mr Hacker. He was a great friend of Dan Brimley and although responsible for the area of Hove North of the railway they also visited together in the new estate at Moulsecoomb. Herbert Hacker was born in Wiltshire to godly parents and became a committed Christian at 12 years of age. He joined the Town Mission in 1933 on a salary of £ 12 a month. He was rarely lost for words and was able to talk freely about his faith. Once he even shared the Gospel with a lady as her dog was biting his hand!

His district included the council estate known as The Knoll. One of the poorest roads at that time was Egremont Road and the children were nick-named 'eggies'. One lady who lived there had five children and when Herbert called two of the girls had TB and the eldest boy was so thin they called him 'barebones'. His main meal of the day which he took to school in a tobacco tin was a piece of bread and dripping or a boiled potato sandwich.

The only furniture upstairs was a double bed in which all the children slept, a single mattress for the lady and an old cupboard with a few clothes in. Downstairs was a rocking chair, two other wooden chairs, a wooden crate which was used as a table, a few cardboard boxes and some chipped crockery.

There was nothing on the floor boards and nothing at the windows, whilst a bare electric light bulb hung in the centre of the living room, usually unlit because there wasn't a shilling to put in the slot meter.

Mr Hacker found clothes for the whole family and brought two more beds from the other end of town on his bicycle, one piece at a time. He arranged for the two girls with TB to be sent to a children's home and for the others to receive free school milk. Over the weeks he found more clothes and eventually work for the lady as a cook in a hostel where she could live with her children. In the end, as a result of the love of God shown in such a practical way, she was attending church regularly.

Another missionary of this period with an interesting background was Stan Warner. He had been born on the Canadian prairies in Southern Saskatchewan. Although his parents were God fearing people, at 13 years of age Stan went to work with a Government road construction gang and there he learned 'all that was evil and nothing good'.

His testimony continues: 'I ran away from home to join the Canadian Army when I was 18 and served my country and the Devil for four years. I then married an English girl before returning to Canada. There we lived for the world and its pleasures until through the overruling hand of God we lost all we had and returned to England in 1923. I went to work next to a Christian boy who was the first person to rebuke me for my foul language. He invited me to the Heathfield Welcome Mission where I was deeply convicted of the selfish life I had been living'.

Stan Warner joined the Mission in 1936 and was especially keen on open air. work. During the war he joined the Open Air Mission for a few years where he spent many hours witnessing to hundreds of Canadian soldiers in the army camps around the country. He eventually rejoined the BHTM and settled in Portslade from where he walked each day to his district around Western Road, Brighton.

All these missionaries were certainly men of character and they needed to be in order to survive in that kind of calling. They supported and encouraged one another in the work and, as well as regular times of prayer and study together there were funny moments too.

There was the time when they were acting as stewards at a Town Mission meeting in the Music Room at the Royal Pavilion. A Mr Russell was always 'in charge'. He liked to make sure that the front rows of chairs were well filled first so he roped off the rear section. He usually wore a tail coat on these occasions, which had a pocket in the 'tail' where he kept the string for this job. This time he removed the string from a section of chairs just before the meeting began. Unknown to him, the end of the ball already in his pocket had been pulled out and caught on a chair. He proceeded to walk down the aisle, across the front of the hall and up the opposite aisle with the ball of string unwinding all the time. Eventually the end was freed but by this time dozens of people were trying not to laugh at the sight of Mr Russell walking around with thirty yards of string trailing behind him.

Chapter Nine

Best of Times, Worst of Times

'It was the best of times, it was the worst of times, it was the age of wisdom, and it was the age of foolishness...'

Charles Dickens (A Tale of Two Cities)

Relief from six years of war came in 1945 with the defeat of Germany then the surrender of Japan. Victory in war however is not true peace. The Committee of the Town Mission recognised that a man-made peace is a mirage and that the work must go on of telling all men everywhere, the need for peace with God.

The years from 1945-1975 saw many changes in national life. Some of these were undoubtedly for the better. This period included the best years of the 'Welfare State' which did much to ease the hardships and uncertainties of life for the poor. The standard of living was to improve dramatically and by the early seventies many homes had consumer goods which were almost unthought of before the war. Televisions, refrigerators, automatic washing machines and a whole range of electrical goods were filling the homes, and the lives, of many people.

Even though times may have been better materially, this period also saw great changes in the attitudes and morals of the nation. Queen Victoria, when asked what had made Britain 'Great' during the 19th century, took a Bible in her hands and said 'This Book'. Over the years, however, God's way to peace and joy was replaced by man's ideas. Even the laws of the land which had been based on the Bible were gradually changed.

One result was an increasing breakdown in family life which was reflected in a soaring divorce rate. Even as Prime Minister Harold Macmillan was declaring in the late 1950's that 'we have never had it so good' the seeds of permissiveness were being sown. During the years that followed, the harvest would include many broken, lonely and frustrated lives.

It was against this background of a changing social fabric that the Town Mission continued its outreach. As the Mission moved towards its centenary, Rev Pitt Bonarjee prepared a history of the work. Rev Bonarjee was a very humble man of Indian origin who served as the minister at the Countess of Huntingdon Church as well as being an important figure on the BHTM Committee. Unfortunately he died suddenly in March 1948 just as his interesting booklet was completed.

One of the things that Rev Bonarjee attempted to do was to calculate the impact that the Mission had made over its first hundred years. He worked out the number of visits made and tracts distributed so that local Christians could appreciate the scale of the work accomplished. He recorded these in round figures and always underestimated numbers so that there was no risk of exaggeration. He estimated that two million house to house visits had been made between 1849 and 1948 with admission into well over one million homes where prayer and scripture reading had taken place. Over three million tracts and half a million Bibles or Gospels had been distributed. During those years over 8,000 open air meetings had been held and 57,000 visits paid to public houses to preach and give out literature.

The centenary was the cause for much rejoicing and thanksgiving to God for maintaining the work over that time. A special service was held at the Countess of Huntingdon Church on June 15th 1949. Gratitude was also expressed in a very practical way through the giving of special Centenary gifts from supporters. This resulted in over £500 being donated which meant that for the first time in a number of years income exceeded expenditure. This was another indication of God's hand upon the work and an encouragement to go into the future looking to the Lord to supply every need.

Provision took another form in 1953 when the Council of Emmanuel Church in Montpelier Place, agreed that the small hall in Lower Market Street, just South of Western Road in Hove, be given to the Town Mission. This served a number of purposes over the next 30 years. It was used as a centre for a children's work and then several of the missioners took responsibility for starting Gospel services and Ladies' meetings and under their guidance and devotion the work grew.

Over the years the Committee had met in various places in order to discuss and pray about the work in which they all had such an interest. At times during the early years there were over 35 members on the Committee and they met every week usually on a Monday morning.

In the 1860' s they met at 31 Western Road which was the local depot for the Religious Tract Society. In the 1880's they had an office in Prince Albert Street and then for many years a room in Steine House also in the heart of Brighton. When this was relinquished around 1940 the Committee met in the vestry of the Countess of Huntingdon Church, usually on a Tuesday morning.

From 1956 the Lower Market Street Mission Hall was used. It was here that the missionaries would come each week to meet the Committee. These occasions were very formal but over the years the relationship between 'employer and employed' became more like that of co-workers in one work. In more recent times the Committee met at the Baptist Tabernacle which had been built on the site of Emmanuel Church on the Brighton and Hove border. In 1989 the monthly Committee meeting was transferred to the new Mission office in Albion Street.

During the 1950's and 1960's, against a tide of apathy, the work of outreach continued. As 1953 was Coronation Year, a special booklet was distributed called 'The Royal Day' . Over the years the missionaries had always used literature like the 'Town Mission Evangelist' or 'Town Mission Herald' to leave in the homes they visited. This special booklet was circulated to hundreds of homes and pointed to Jesus as King of Kings.

Each month over 5,000 Scripture Union magazines were distributed on the housing estates to children and teenagers; Bible Reading Notes were also provided for the adults. Permission was also granted to witness at the race-course and several of the missionaries went to distribute literature and hold open air meetings on the Race Hill.

Wherever possible the missionaries worked in conjunction with local churches in the work of sharing the Gospel. They also helped during crusades and campaigns where Christ was exalted and the Gospel preached. During 1963 and especially during the 'All Britain Billy Graham Crusade' of 1967, some of the missioners were involved. Night after night at The Dome they helped with the counselling and saw many encouraging and lasting conversions.

The door to door visiting, however, was still the main work and although attitudes were hardening, there were still some remarkable reports of lives revolutionised by a knock at the door from a Town Missioner. As one door was opened by an elderly lady the missioner caught a glimpse of another lady sick in bed in the back room. After introducing himself and stating the purpose of his visit he was told to go away as 'we don't want religion here'!

The sad state of these two sisters played on the missionary's mind and so next day he went to a flower shop. He returned to the house with a flower arrangement. This time the response was rather different because on seeing the flowers he was summoned into the back room to see the sick lady. In time this act of love resulted in both ladies coming to Christ.

In 1963 the Town Mission broke new ground by appointing a lady to the missionary staff. To some, visiting could be seen as too demanding and too dangerous to be conducted by ladies. However, there were often situations where it was difficult for the men to counsel, especially as those most likely to be at home during the day were women.

Miss Stone who was attached to Bishop Hannington Church, Hove, was appointed and did an excellent job of visiting in that area. Another female appointment was Mrs Matsell, whose husband, Charlie, was the missionary in charge at Lower Market Street. In 1977 two ladies from Woodingdean, Miss Hayward and Miss Hurst also served the Mission for a short time. The last woman to be employed was Mrs Tomsett who was appointed to her home area in Whitehawk in 1979.

Hospital visitation and especially a ministry to the sick and dying has always been an important part of the work. Many a lonely person has died with only a Town Missioner to care and be by the bedside. Bevendean Hospital, the Brighton General and the Sussex County Hospital were visited regularly as were many homes for the elderly. Where possible, short services were arranged and some of these became part of the missioners' 'routine'.

One area of hospital work which is seldom thought of is that of visiting sick children. On returning from the forces in 1946, a young man was taken along to the Royal Alexandra Children's Hospital in Brighton by his father. They went along to cheer the children up through music and by sharing stories, using a flannelgraph. Life in hospital in those days was grim and the rules strict, so the children appreciated the efforts of their Christian visitors.

The young man accompanying his father was Ron Bridle. He was so taken with this work that today, over 40 years later, he is still visiting weekly and although hospital conditions are vastly different, the need to tell of the love of Jesus is just the same.

A number of years after meeting Mr Bridle in the Children's Hospital, a lady wrote to him explaining how she had left hospital determined to find out more about the Christian faith. She had gone on not only to serve Christ but also to teach others what she knew. Ron Bridle eventually joined the Town Mission in 1966 and incorporated the visits to the Children's Hospital into his new work.

'Uncle Ron's' love and concern for children also found an expression through the 'Sunshine Club'. This was a monthly paper containing quizzes and scripture verses which was sent to children throughout the area. At one time over 300 children were in the Sunshine Club and as many of the youngsters came from non-Christian families it was a wonderful opportunity to get the Word of God into homes.

During the early years, meetings were also arranged several times a year. During the summer these would be in the park on the Knoll Estate, Hove, or in Aldrington Church during the Christmas holidays. At a time when young people were hearing less and less about the Christian message in their schools, this work amongst children was of the utmost importance.

By the early 1970's the Town Mission had come through a time when despite many encouragements the work was in need of a fresh impetus to meet the challenge of the age. Some of God's faithful servants were reaching the end of their years of service. In 1970 Mr Waldron celebrated over 50 years in the work. During part of that time he had had the responsibility for Islingword Road Mission as well as being a missionary and Secretary to the Town Mission.

In 1974 another long serving member of the Committee died. Wilfred Dillistone had served as Treasurer since 1941 and during his years in office he had taken the responsibility for the Mission's finances very personally. With the passing of two such long-standing Committee members, changes were inevitable and one of the oldest Christian outreaches in the area was about to enter a new phase.

Chapter Ten

Fresh Winds.

By the 1970's the face of Brighton had changed. An area south of Western Road which had suffered badly from bombing during the war had been developed into a large shopping complex. This was Churchill Square whose open piazzas would be much used over the years by every kind of busker and pavement artist and, more importantly, for open air preaching. The skyline had been pierced by several 'sky scrapers' such as Sussex Heights and the character of the sea front had been altered by the building of an entertainments centre and then a large conference centre.

The Town Mission was also going through a time of change. This was expressed in the Chairman's 1978 report. "This Mission is not a 'has been' and the revitalising energy of the Holy Spirit has, we now believe, given us the springboard for expansion in the future; we must increase our missionary strength with young people with a vision for souls." The heart's desire of the Committee and supporters for younger missioners was to be fulfilled in the years that followed.

Over the next decade God, brought into the work young men who were willing to leave good secular jobs to serve the Lord in the Mission. They had a zeal for evangelism and wanted to use their individual gifts in the work of the Gospel. The make-up of the team had a more balanced look with a mixture of younger and older men and women. The needs of Brighton and Hove were immense and the population as diverse as any in England and so a balanced and enthusiastic team was vital if the Mission was to prosper.

Times had changed and the Mission had to be flexible in its approach without compromising the truth of the Gospel or departing from its basic principles. Long gone were the days when there were streets full of children playing on the pavements without fear. Also both parents might now be at work during the day, leaving housing estates quiet or deserted. The community spirit of pre-war years had decayed and more mobile population made it difficult to build relationships.

As the standard of living had improved, the need to provide practical help became less vital. Some agencies were doing an excellent work amongst the poor but few were addressing man's deepest need which was to come into a relationship with their God and Father. Given the spiritual poverty of the age, the Mission had to concentrate its efforts on sharing the Gospel in a direct way with the population.

Adapting to the changing times, the missionaries continued to take their message out to the people. The schools' work grew and provided a

Part of Albion Hill Redevelopment

wonderful opportunity to present Christ to children who had no contact with the Christian faith. Up to 200 children could be reached during an assembly, as well as their teachers.

During the holidays 'Adventure Clubs' were arranged with local churches and this was another way of contacting youngsters and their parents. At the other end of the educational system, Christian students and lecturers at the University of Sussex were contacted and a prayer group developed there.

During the 1980's momentous news was filling the headlines. There was the Falklands War and the dispute with the miners. On October 12th 1984 Brighton was flung onto the front page of the newspapers. An IRA bomb had been planted in the Grand Hotel on the Brighton seafront. It had been planned to kill delegates who were in town for the Conservative Party conference. At 2.54 am it exploded and ripped a huge hole in the front of the stately hotel. The main target of the bomb, Prime Minister Margaret Thatcher, escaped injury and lived to fight another day. However five people were killed and scores injured. Such were the times in which people were living and it was against this background of disputes and instability that the Mission worked.

From time to time there was an opportunity to get involved with those in trouble with the law. In the early 1980's a young Brighton lad was arrested for murder. The Town Mission contacted his parents and they were pleased to receive advice and support. This contact resulted in several evangelistic meetings being arranged at the detention centre in Reigate with up to 25 young offenders listening to the Gospel. Visits were also made to Lewes prison. This was mainly to encourage a number of West African men who had requested a visit and wanted to do some Bible studies.

Jesus told His followers to "Go into all the world and preach the Gospel." During the summer months all the world seemed to descend on Brighton in the form of tourists and language students. Up to 12,000 students were in the area each week and many stayed with local families. They came mostly from the EEC countries but some came from as far away as Japan, Mexico and the Middle East. Here again was an opportunity for ministry.

Open Air work in the 'Old' Churchill Square

Several of the missionaries became involved in open air work in the Churchill Square precinct and important contacts were made. At times a book table offering free books and gospels was used to attract people and there were also open air meetings using a sketch-board as a focus. On one occasion a missionary was having his lunch when he got into conversation with two young men from Turkey. The missionary shared about the Lord and just as the students were leaving he reached into his bag and pulled out two Gospels in Turkish which he happened to have with him! This God-given opening is all the more remarkable when one considers that Turkey is one of the least evangelised nations in the world and it emphasised again the great opportunities there are right on our doorstep.

One of the reasons for the vitality that now characterised the Mission was the enthusiasm generated by its Secretary, Rev.

Fred Money. He had been involved as a missionary for over 10 years and he understood every aspect of the work. During his time as Secretary from 1977 to 1986 his outgoing personality and willingness to serve helped to build bridges with local Christians and churches. This in turn widened the support for the work not only in the Brighton area, but throughout Sussex.

One of the new events that was introduced during Rev. Money's time was the 'Gift Day.' Over the years part of the finances needed for the work had been raised from a 'Sale of Work.' This had been held in a large hall like the old Hove Town Hall and everyone rallied round to make it a success. However, as times were changing it seemed more appropriate to organise an opportunity for supporters to hear more about the work and to bring a practical gift towards the expenses incurred. The first Gift Day was held in 1979 and this step of faith was justified as giving was four times that raised from the last Sale of Work.

In 1982 the old mission hall in Lower Market Street was sold, which meant that the Mission had no official head-quarters. There was a real need for a large room in the centre of Brighton which could serve as an office and prayer room. In 1988 prayer was answered in a wonderful way. The Elim Church was moving out of the Lanes to a new Church Centre in Albion Street adjacent to St. Peter's Church. They kindly offered the Mission the use of a room in their new building which was then equipped as an administration centre and counselling room. The new headquarters was also situated right in the heart of the area where the Town Missionaries had begun visiting nearly 140 years earlier.

Brighton Station has always played an important part in the success and prosperity of the area. By the 1980's over 12 million passengers a year were passing through. With this in mind a Poster Campaign was started in 1988 and large hoarding rented on the main London platform. The poster contained some thought provoking words together with a scripture text and the address of the Mission. The poster provided an excellent opportunity to present the Word of God for 24 hours a day right in the heart of the town. A few years later the Mission took this idea one stage further by having a similar scheme with texts placed on the buses of Brighton and Hove.

One of the aims of the Mission over the years was to work alongside the local church in evangelism. Clearly a few missionaries attempting to make an impact on a vast area is an impossible task, especially when some statistics are considered.

In the 1880's when the population was still around 100,000 the ratio of missionaries to population was about 1:18,000. As districts were so much smaller at that time and society far less mobile, real friendships could develop. By the 1980's the ratio was one missioner to around 60,000 people.

This highlighted the need to see churches and individual Christians getting involved in evangelism. The Town Mission began encouraging people to join in the work. During the summer some special weeks of outreach were organised when volunteers received some basic training and went out visiting or helping with open air meetings. This venture was called 'Breakout' as it was helping churches and individuals to break out of the churches with the Gospel message. Indeed back in 1880 groups of local Christians were also linking up with some missionaries in a similar way and helping with street meetings and preaching on the Fish Market Hard.

By the end of the 1980's Brighton and Hove was a busy cosmopolitan town and the task facing the whole Body of Christ could not be underestimated. Every form of belief, sin and perversion could be found in the towns and the forces of evil had a firm hold. It was now 140 years since the Town Mission had been inaugurated and the need to go 'into the streets and lanes' with the message of Life was as vital as ever.

Chapter Eleven.

In a Land Far Away.

During 1991, over a thousand miles. from Brighton, an event was taking place which was to shape the future of the mission. In the Sudan, the rise of extremist Moslem groups resulted in up to four million citizens fleeing the country. The majority of the Sudanese people identified with one of the Christian denominations. They were forced to leave everything behind and many came to Britain. They arrived in a foreign land with little prospect of returning home.

Within a few months several hundred Sudanese had re-located to Brighton or Hove. The main reason why so many came to this area was because a small core of Sudanese people already lived in the towns. They were able to give help with resettlement and with finding accommodation. The arrival of 150 new families would be a challenge to the local churches and to the Town Mission.

As usual God had gone ahead and prepared the way for a significant and encouraging work. During the early part of 1991 the Mission had seen the need to develop a 'project based approach' to outreach. With only five or six full time workers trying to reach out to a population of 250,000 it seemed right to seek God through prayer as to where to concentrate the effort. The committee were keen to build on the strengths and interests of each worker. There was also a vision to encourage the local churches and Christians to get more involved in the vast task of evangelism across the towns. Over the years that followed, several God given projects were started by the Mission and grew into significant ministries.

One of these projects was a work which became known as the 'Sudanese Project'. God's sovereign hand was on this venture from the start. It began when a new worker was appointed who was Arab speaking and had a wealth of experience in dealing with ethnic groups. Phillip Deuk had recently joined the team from Birmingham where he had been a manager at Cadbury's before training at Birmingham Bible College. He had worked amongst Moslems and Arabic speaking people. He had just the right gifts, personality and linguistic skills for the task ahead. Phillip was already working amongst the local Arabic community in Brighton and Hove and had set up several Bible studies before events in North Africa gave the work a fresh dimension.

When working amongst specific people groups such as students, Moslems or members of the deaf community, the first step is to identify with the group. Each group has its own culture which needs to be understood so that bridges can be built and relationships developed. Phillip was able to come alongside the Sudanese refugees and understand their pressures and worries. They were in an alien culture and were often living in crowded and sub-standard accommodation. The first priority was to care for the group and show practical support during their time of trouble.

Any contact had to be sensitive to their background and beliefs. Phillip could speak their language and he understood their culture. His own church was adjacent to the main part of town where the majority of the Sudanese lived. Soon church members were coming into contact with the Sudanese, particularly through the local schools. Some of the new arrivals were evangelical Christians and they quickly linked up with local churches. The vast majority, however, were Coptic Christians with a more orthodox style of worship. The main question became "What was the best way to reach out to the group?"

The first step was to show love and practical help to a community who were feeling lost and traumatised by their experiences. Phillip's initial form of practical help was an 'Advisory Forum.' Local business men and professionals were contacted. Some were accountants, some solicitors and some were working in career guidance. A forum was set up in a local hall with a panel of these experts giving their time free of charge. They were able to answer questions on issues like housing, employment and benefits and to give more personal help if required. This was a successful first step which showed the love of Christ through the local church in action.

What was needed now was a more specific way of breaking down the barriers and drawing the group closer to Christ. Much prayer was given as to how to take the 'Sudanese Project' forward. The whole work exploded when it was realised that the greatest need was for this group to learn English. Again it was God's providence that Phillip had just completed a course in 'Teaching English as a Foreign Language.' He also had links with a Christian language school which provided teaching material that was Bible based. The Elders at Phillip's church quickly made church rooms available free of charge. The work was ready to take off.

One of the aims of the Mission was to motivate and encourage local Christians in reaching out for Christ. Too many Christians were merely spectators in their churches and there seemed to be a wealth of talent waiting to be used for God's glory. The need for help with the Sudanese people and in particular the need for teachers, led to the involvement of many Christians from different local churches. These volunteers came from every age group. They came from a variety of backgrounds including ex-teachers, missionaries and nurses. Other Christians were involved in catering, transport and preparing material at home. Here then, was the body of Christ in action, showing practical love and sharing the Gospel.

There were six classes in total. Some were held in the morning and some in the evening. A small fee was charged towards the books and materials. There were three levels of teaching according to ability. Each student was given an Arab/English New Testament which became the main reader for the course. Eventually over 300 bi-lingual New Testaments were distributed, all paid for by local churches. Within two months there were twelve teachers and eighty Sudanese in the classes.

The project developed in several ways. Social events, like dances, were held to build bridges with the wider Sudanese community. A mid-week Arabic Bible study was started. During the summer of 1992 a special week of events and concerts were held with visiting Christian speakers and singers. Over 250 Sudanese attended these events. As a result of all these meetings over sixty people made a commitment to Christ and the Bible study group grew dramatically.

The project ran in this form for over two years until 1994. By then several hundred Sudanese had passed through the classes. As the community became established there was no longer the need to learn English. The Sudanese became more 'at home' in the area and were becoming a part of the local community. A Coptic church serving the needs of some of the group was established. Many others joined Evangelical churches and the mid-week Bible study continued. There were still opportunities to serve the group in practical ways and more formally with counselling and pastoral care.

There was much encouragement in all this for the Brighton and Hove Town Mission and lessons for the future growth of its mission to the twin towns. Although the Sudanese Project was used by God for a specific time it is clear that the long term effect of the work was more far reaching than the original project envisaged. This had indeed been a great missionary opportunity. It showed that local Christians and local missions must be alert to changes and new approaches to mission. The church was seen as relevant and in step with the specific needs of the time. Christians were empowered and released to serve God in new ways. The project expressed the heart of God in caring for the poor and the stranger in the land. It showed the love of Christ in healing broken lives and reaching out in practical ways. It showed the power of the Gospel to bring new life and hope to all who respond to its call.

Chapter Twelve.

Towards the Millennium.

The decade of the 1990's was to see many changes at the Town Mission and God was sowing seeds which were to bear fruit in the new millennium. At this time City Missions across the country, and indeed the world, were seeing the urgency and importance of their work. In Birmingham, Edwin Orton had led the Birmingham City Mission into a new and exciting phase. He then applied his enthusiasm to creating a British Association of City Missions and in 1991 an inaugural conference was held at the new Birmingham Convention Centre. The local mission in Brighton was one of the co-founders of this growing association and in May 1992 Edwin spoke to over 200 Town Mission supporters who gathered at Hove Town Hall for the Spring Convention and Gift Day. The Mayor of Hove gave the welcome and the whole event was a truly memorable occasion.

Along with the successful Sudanese Project, this period in the Mission's history also saw the establishment of the Schools Project. For over two decades Ron Bridle had taken school assemblies on behalf of the Mission. 'Uncle Ron' retired in 1991 and it now seemed to be the right time to take this work forward. Tony Smith had recently given up a successful business as a photographer to join the Mission. One of his burdens was for the schools and the thousands of youngsters in the area. In May 1991, a small number of interested teachers, parents and prayer partners met at Albion Street for the launch of the 'Schools Project.' Their prayer for a full time worker was soon to be answered.

Carol Boreham had been brought up in Henfield and had been teaching mathematics at Kings Manor School in Shoreham when she felt God prompting her to become a full time schools worker for the Mission. She started in September 1992 and soon the work blossomed. She linked up with other schools workers and built up a team which not only took assemblies but also started running lunch time clubs in schools. She also spoke in many RE lessons and was invited to share a Christian perspective in PSE (Personal and Social Education) lessons. Under Carol's leadership the schools work grew quickly. By the time she left to start a family in 1994, she had laid a strong foundation and passed on her expertise and vision to people like Jon Bebb who were then used to take the work forward.

Changes were happening in every area of the Mission in the first half of the 1990's. Berni Bannier left in 1993 to take on the leadership of the Goldstone Church in Hove. Ron Pittfield, who had been the chairman of the committee since 1977, passed on this role to Ray Wingate. The Elim Church needed to extend their work at the Albion Street premises and so the Mission office moved to the Ebenezer Chapel, a mere hundred yards away. At this time Harold Oakley took on the role as Administrator. This happened at a time when the Mission was becoming a registered Charity and Harold had just the skills to lead the Mission through this minefield of administration. By the end of 1996 Harold's work was complete and Tony Smith was appointed acting General Secretary.

Throughout this time of change, the work of sharing the Gospel continued. Missioners worked at taking the Good News of Jesus to the homes and onto the streets of the twin Towns. One of these workers was a young man who had come down from his home in the Lake District to answer God's call. Paul Bingham had a thick Cumbrian accent and a heart for the poor and desperate. He visited some of the neediest people of the area including those living in the Kingswood and Milner Flats. Day or night Paul was there to help in practical ways and always ready to share his love for Christ. His journal was full of reports which showed how sacrificial love can lead to openings for the Gospel. This following story is typical of his work.

"I went along to the local council flats to see if I could be of help during some bitterly cold weather. When I came across the bed-sit of Reg and Betty it was like entering a Victorian slum. The room was dark, not just because the curtains were always closed, but because of years of grime. The only visible form of warmth was the double bed in which this elderly couple spent their days. Even the poor lighting couldn't hide the soiled grey bed clothes that covered them. Yet there they stayed day after day. She was blind and he had arthritis. To tell them that God loved them seemed such an inadequate thing to say and yet that was all they needed to hear to cause them to open their hearts. They prayed a simple prayer of repentance and asked Jesus to be their Saviour and Lord. That dark dingy room suddenly became a delightful place where Jesus was pleased to stay."

There were lighter moments too. Having knocked on a lady's door, the visitor then asked if she went to church. "Of course" she replied, "I've been going to church for 25 years." The missioner remarked how marvellous this was and then asked if she believed in God. "Certainly not!" she replied. Another amusing comment was overheard when an 'alien' missioner was invited into a home. A voice called out from the back room "You shouldn't let strange men into the house." The interesting reply was "Oh it's alright. He's not a real man!"

As the Mission prepared for the Millennium its aim was to present the unchanging Christ to a changing society. Any and every means were used to get the Good News of Jesus out to the people. There were times of linking up with the Open Air Campaigners to share on the streets. On September 4th 1998 a new shopping mall was opened on the Churchill Square site. Over 70 new shops together with restaurants and cafes filled the concrete and glass structure. The new high security shopping centre made open airs impossible on this site and so the search was on for new places to contact people and to preach. The Pavilion Gardens became a good venue to meet local people as well as visitors and language students. Brighton was still a thriving centre for teaching English to foreign students and there were great opportunities to spread the Word of God across the world through these students. It was at this time that the Mission started to acquire Gospels and other Christian literature in a variety of languages. One Gospel booklet called 'Ultimate Questions' was available in 30 languages. These excellent resources became a permanent feature of the Mission's outreach. A mother requested a Tibetan Gospel for her daughter-in-law who was a Buddhist. She was encouraged to read and meditate on God's Word. Some weeks later an excited mother contacted the Mission to say that her daughter–in-law had found faith in Christ.

Away from the hustle and bustle of the streets, the Gospel was also being shared in quieter corners. For many years, Missioners had visited Residential Homes for the elderly. Sometimes short meetings were held and helpers from local churches came to share in the work. Week after week, Residential Homes like Caburn House were visited by a faithful group of Christians. Even on Christmas Day speakers from the Town Mission or local churches were there to point to the Saviour. Volunteers like Yvonne Davenport built up contacts with many homes. Her winning nature opened many doors and she established regular Gospel services across the area. Little did these small teams know that within a few years this concern for the elderly was to grow into an even bigger work

As the Millennium approached there were signs that the spiritual temperature in the towns was rising. Tony Smith, as General Secretary, was always keen to reach out into new areas and in new ways with the Gospel. He developed the outreach into the community under the banner of 'Lifeline' and introduced new ideas for sharing the Gospel. He had a vision for a fresh work in the difficult Whitehawk Estate which had the reputation, both locally and nationally, of being a challenging area. According to some statistics the estate had the highest incidence of substance misuse in England. However at the heart of the estate God was at work. There was a small group of Christians living there who were prepared to get involved with the community. Some of the Town Mission's early initiatives in the area were to result in a significant work for God in the years that followed.

Other estates benefited from the work of the team. On the Knoll Estate in Hove a weekly coffee and fellowship morning was started to encourage the small number of Christians living there. The tough north Hangleton area saw a season of real blessing as a Christian home facilitated weekly and sometimes, twice weekly meetings. The Bible was taught often through a veil of cigarette smoke and it powerfully touched the lives of both believers and unbelievers. Those gatherings were affectionately known as the 'Whosoevers.'

Martin Halliday and Mike McNally in Hollingdean

The poverty and material needs that were evident in some homes was beginning to raise questions about the role of the Mission. It could be that God was prompting a return to the roots of the work which had thrived back in Victorian times. It was through meeting physical and material needs that the love of God for the poor was shown in practical ways. Tony did not know, at this stage, that within a few years this seed of an idea was to grow into a vibrant work which became known as the 'Basics Bank.'

Tony was also keen to link up with other evangelists and with the local Evangelical Alliance to promote the Gospel. One joint initiative was a Gospel meeting for business people called 'Lunch Time with a Difference.' This was based at the Royal

Albion Hotel near the sea front. Sandwiches were provided for people taking a break from their office or shop. As they relaxed, a short Gospel talk was given, together with a challenge to follow Christ.

In 1999 the Town Mission celebrated 150 years since its inauguration. Over this time God had provided for His work in response to the prayers of His people. Prayer has always been a central pillar in the growth of the Mission. An enthusiastic group of volunteers came together every three months to help with the mail out to supporters. A quarterly newsletter together with a prayer diary was sent to up to 1,000 prayer partners. It has been the fervent prayer of faithful Christians which has kept the Mission moving in the will of God. Regular meetings for prayer were also arranged in homes across the towns.

There have been many answers to the prayers of God's people. On one occasion a prayer request was being brought before God. It concerned the need for an administrator to help in the office. Just as the 'Amen' was uttered there was a knock on the door. A gentleman came in who had recently been made redundant. This turned out to be Maurice Blundell who was a mature Christian and a skilled administrator. He had felt God prompting him to offer his services to the Mission as a volunteer. Needless to say his offer was accepted and he served faithfully for a number of years.

By the side of the River Thames the huge white structure of the Millennium Dome was now complete. The nation and the world waited expectantly for the 'Big Ben' to strike midnight. As the country entered the year 2000 there was an air of optimism that this could be a new era of prosperity and peace. However the euphoria was to be short lived. The problems of a modern society were soon evident for all to see. Around the corner was the additional horror of terrorism on a new scale.

As the 20th century was drawing to a close the Brighton and Hove Town Mission was determined to continue its God-given work of declaring the Good News of Jesus across the area. Thousands of special Millennium Gospels were prepared for distribution across both Towns. For over 150 years the Brighton and Hove Town Mission had continued the work of sharing the Gospel. As a new century and a new Millennium dawned the opposition to the authority of Christ and His Word would be just as strong. However, the promise from the Scriptures was that the Gospel was still the 'power of God for salvation to all who believe.' The challenge for the Mission was whether it could continue to meet the needs of the age in the new Millennium.

Chapter Thirteen.

New City, New Challenges.

To mark both the new Millennium and the forthcoming Golden Anniversary of Queen Elizabeth's Accession to the throne, it was announced that suitably qualified towns would be granted city status. In February 2001, the mayor received notice that the twin towns of Brighton and Hove would indeed become a city and so the Town Mission became the Brighton and Hove City Mission. The authorities and dignitaries of the new 'City by the Sea' were excited by the prospect of a prosperous future for the City of Brighton and Hove. For Tony and the Trustees working at the Mission, the personal problems and struggles of many of the local residents were just as great as ever and needed addressing.

The Mission had a new Chairman ready to take the work forward. John Prideaux, a chemistry teacher at Brighton College, had been on the Council of the Mission for a number of years when in 1999 he became Chairman. Over the next few years he would oversee several new initiatives including the move in February 2000 to a new Headquarters at the Methodist Church building in London Road.

Week by week the task of contacting young and old continued. As well as the work in the local schools there were other initiatives with young people. The work on the Whitehawk estate was gathering pace with clubs for young people held at venues like St. David's Hall and the local Community Centre. A Christian businessman had taken over the Whitehawk Inn and had changed the building into a centre for teaching computer technology to the local community. Summer play schemes were organised and there were links with the successful Kidz Klub. Tireless workers including Clive Manning, Mike McNally and Luana Hall, who all had a real heart for the people of the area, were totally involved with the community. They saw clubs such as the Big Breakthrough Club and Friday Club flourish. Luana's contact with the mothers of some of the children would eventually lead her to form 'Life Stream.' The aim was to support young mothers in need of refreshment week by week and especially to provide occasional weekends away at a country retreat.

On the world stage dramatic events were taking place. September 11th 2001, was one of those momentous days which stay forever etched in the mind. Like the assassination of John F. Kennedy in 1963, it was to become an infamous date that will have powerful memories for all who lived through such an event. The sight of the two planes ripping into the Twin Towers in New York on that perfect early autumn morning is an image few can ever forget. The unleashing of such evil, which led to massive death and destruction, shook the world.

One question the terror attack raised was 'Where was God on September 11th?' As the world looked for answers, it was John Blanchard, a national evangelist, who wrote a brilliant gospel booklet with that title, pointing the reader to Christ. John Blanchard was later to become a member of the Mission Council of Reference and also spoke at a Mission event in Hove in 2005. Tony Smith quickly saw an evangelistic opportunity as the world

JOHN BLANCHARD
AUTHOR OF THE AWARD WINNING *DOES GOD BELIEVE IN ATHEISTS?*

WHERE WAS GOD ON SEPTEMBER 11?

The answer may surprise you....
Return this card today
for a FREE copy of this book

looked for answers. The Mission printed 60,000 post cards which had a stark colour picture of the burning twin towers on the front and an invitation to write in for a free copy of John Blanchard's booklet.

The post cards were distributed by 21 local churches to homes across the city. The response was most encouraging. Over 360 requests for the book arrived at the Mission office and these in turn were followed up by local churches.

The Rev. Fred Money was the President of the Mission and although well into his 70's, he was still working for his Lord wherever he could. He had read in the national press about the trial of Jonathan Aitken. Jonathan had been a Conservative Member of Parliament whose career was so successful that some political commentators expected him to be Prime Minister one day. However his meteoric rise came to an abrupt end when he was sentenced to a term in prison for perjury. Fred wrote to Jonathan and a correspondence developed between them. The result was that a new, humble, Jonathan Aitken came to speak at a Mission event at Brighton Marina. This took the form of a men's breakfast where a large gathering of men heard the story of a man whose experiences had led him from prison to praise.

Sadly, Fred died in July 2006. His radiance and love for His Lord must have influenced thousands of people over the years. On the estates of Bevendean, Moulsecoomb and Hollingdean and across other areas of Brighton and Hove he shared his faith with everyone. Fred's cheery greeting and winning smile was hard to resist. Many came to the Lord through his testimony. He was also prepared to roll up his sleeves and show his love for Christ in practical ways. One very icy morning he was seen wheeling a barrow load of coal up a steep hill to a needy home. Even in his last years when he survived a heart attack, his first words were, "The Lord's spared me so there must be more work for me to do." Fred was a rare character who was a blessing to all who knew him.

From 2005 the work of the Mission seemed to take a leap forward. The years of faithful evangelism together with the prayer backing of hundreds of prayer partners resulted in both a widening and a deepening of the ministry. More and more volunteers were coming alongside the paid staff and were helping the outreach to grow. Some of these volunteers were local students or retired people who wanted to serve God. A regular succession of volunteers under the auspices of Care Force joined the work for one year from countries such as Bolivia, India, Kenya, Cameroon and Uganda. The whole team at the City Mission began to see new doors opening for the Gospel and some long-standing areas of outreach like the schools ministry was ready for expansion.

Over the years Brighton has had a reputation for being unconventional and for attracting people with different ideas. This is reflected in the huge 'Wholeness' exhibitions which were held in the city from time to time. This is a gathering of every kind of 'spiritual' outlook including witchcraft and alternative therapies. Tony Smith and the team saw this as an opening for the Gospel. They realised that people visiting this event in their thousands would be searching for the answer to life and be spiritually hungry. When the 'Body, Mind and Soul' exhibition opened at the Brighton Race Course conference centre, the Mission had an exhibit right in the centre. The Mission linked up with five local churches and manned a stall at the heart of the exhibition. There were many opportunities to share Christ and pray with visitors.

Another new avenue for ministry was called 'Open Door.' Martin Halliday had linked up with the Mission over many years to help with various projects. He felt God lead him to volunteer at a drop-in centre for those with Aids/HIV which was located in Kemp Town. People would call in at 'Open Door' for a cup of tea and a chat. This was a sensitive work and Martin was just the right person to offer a listening ear and support to those in need. When this phase of his work came to a close in 2007, Martin then moved on to help with 'Voices in Exile' giving support to refugees and asylum seekers.

The leap forward in the way God used the City Mission was especially evident in the explosion of the schools work. Jon Bebb had served with the Mission as both volunteer and schools worker for over ten years. Together with his wife Beccy they had stood before thousands of youngsters and told them about Jesus. Now they felt called to start a specialist ministry amongst children and young people. Linda Bolton who had been helping as a volunteer with assemblies since 1998 was now appointed as a schools worker. It was 2005 and her first move was to give a new name 'Kids Count' to this ministry. The name was a statement of truth; that children did count in the eyes of God and every individual was precious. Linda passionately believed that 'teaching children to count is not as important as teaching them what counts.'

Kids Count Assembly

Linda's communication skills and her enthusiasm for sharing with children helped her to gain entrance into more and more schools. She was able to build up a team of volunteers to enable this expansion to take place. Soon she was involved in 18 Primary schools from Southwick to Lewes. These developments included new Christian clubs where the children came along to learn about the Bible during their lunch break. Hundreds of Bibles were given out to those showing real interest, and both churches and individuals were trained and encouraged by Linda's ministry.

Linda was typical of the quality of staff that God had provided for the Mission. Not only did she have her own deeply founded faith but she had technical and artistic skills which could be used to get the message of Jesus across in a relevant and compelling way. She had great drive and dedication and never tired in her belief that children do count. Linda's contribution to the annual Partnership Events helped all the supporters to understand the importance of the Mission's role. A supporter who attended one of these meetings at Holland Road Baptist Church was so impressed that they sent a letter to the "The Argus." They wrote: 'Hearing the reports from the team and the testimonies of those being helped really highlighted what the City Mission is all about – lives being changed by the love of Christ. One young lady who was sharing her own story broke down and wept as she was overcome by the love she had received.'

Chapter Fourteen.

A Tale of Two Cities.

One had been opened in 1866. The other opened in 1899. Both had become symbols of Brighton and Hove recognised around the world. These were the two piers that dominated the sea front. Almost as famous as the onion shaped dome of the Royal Pavilion, Brighton's two piers, the Palace Pier and the West Pier, had been notable landmarks for over one hundred years. Millions had visited and photographed them. The Palace Pier was built as 'an amusement and pleasure emporium' and was considered the finest pier in England. The peak of its popularity came in 1939 when there were two million visitors including 45,000 on just one Bank Holiday.

Brighton West Pier 1913 & 2003

By the 1990's things were changing. The West Pier had been structurally unsafe for a number of years and had been closed to the public until funds could be found to renovate it. However, storm damage and a fire resulted in the West Pier becoming a skeleton of wrecked iron work which looked a sad site on the Brighton and Hove border. Whilst the West Pier became the 'sad old lady of the sea,' the Palace Pier, by contrast, was thriving. It controversially had its name changed to the Brighton Pier and with its assortment of funfair rides and other entertainments continued to attract thousands of visitors every week.

The city may have been famous for its two piers but what a contrast between the two. They clearly reflected the extremes of the City they served. One pier was thriving, prosperous and seemed to have a certain future. The other was a wreck with no hope of resurrection. These piers were a parable of a city where some districts featured in the top ten in Britain for affluence whilst other areas were in the top ten for poverty and deprivation. They reflected a city that has both 'up and outs' and 'down and outs'. The truth is that both groups need Christ. Those working for the City Mission were made aware of these great contrasts in society on a daily basis. The front line workers were involved with both kinds of people. It is because all people need to hear the Gospel that the Mission was involved in such a variety of ministries.

One of these ministries was to the elderly. There are many residential and nursing homes in the area, and throughout its history the Mission has visited some of these homes and provided Christian meetings. This work was to expand rapidly from 2006 when God provided a 70 year old grandmother from South Africa to head up this work. Colleen Hurd had been a Christian since her teens and spent her life serving God in various ways. She believed God had now called her to spend some time in England. The door opened for her to work with the City Mission and to develop the ministry among the elderly in Rest Homes. Colleen soon won the confidence of managers and staff and more and more homes opened up. The result was a short Christian service in increasing numbers of homes across the City and an opportunity to comfort and share with many lonely and needy people. A team of volunteers was soon formed to cope with the growing work. 'Treasured Moments' had now become another significant work for God through the City Mission.

Another major ministry was to be the 'Basics Bank.' Despite the obvious wealth in the area, there were still significant pockets of deprivation and poverty. At various times in the history of the Mission the love of Christ had been shown in practical ways. Food had been given to the hungry and basic household items had been provided to those trying to build their first home after coming off the streets. Even at the start of the 21st Century people required help. There were thousands of people in genuine need of practical help. Some of those people were asylum seekers and others homeless or in temporary accommodation. Some were escaping domestic violence and some were ex-prisoners. A growing number were teenagers who were simply turned out of the home and told to fend for themselves. The Biblical mandate to care for the poor, the needy, the widow and the orphan was clear. Tony Smith recognised God's call to rekindle this part of the Mission's work, and several small initiatives to meet the vast need had been started in recent years. It was now time for a big need across the City to be met by an even bigger response.

As far back as the winter of 1996 God had been preparing the ground for this fresh outreach into the community. It was then that Trevor Smetham had been seconded to the Mission from his Bible College in South Wales where he was studying. Almost ten years later Trevor returned to the Mission, with his wife Jill, and their work together resulted in an explosion in the size and effectiveness of the Basics Bank. Part of the impetus for the new phase of this work came from the vision of Jenny Elton.
The story of Jenny and John Elton is one of great contrast and tremendous hope. Back in the 1980's Jenny had to cope with an alcoholic husband whose drinking led to a collapse of his

business. Consequently things became desperate as there were three children to feed and they had no money. Jenny turned to God in prayer. Some local Christians became aware of their plight and began to provide practical support at what was the lowest point of their lives. As time passed God was at work in their situation.

If we fast forward some 20 years to the year 2000 we see a miracle had taken place. John was no longer an alcoholic but a dedicated follower of Jesus. Not only was John a Christian but he was now working for the Mission and faithfully visiting from door to door to share his faith. It was around this time that Jenny heard of the work of a Basics Bank successfully operating in Southampton. She had the vision to see a similar ministry in the Brighton area. Jenny had proved how powerful practical love can be to change the hardest situation and she was keen to see the Mission develop this work.

Around this time Tony and the Trustees were becoming increasingly aware of the hardship of many in the City. What was the point of trying to share the Gospel if someone was hungry or cold? Something needed to be done to meet their needs. As the jigsaw of an expanding Basics Bank fell into place, another indication was the relocation of the Mission Office. In 2000 it took on new premises at the Methodist Church building in London Road. Here they had more space for sorting and storing supplies for the emerging Basics Bank.

Over the next couple of years input from Mission workers like Sue Nunn and Julie Carroll resulted in good contacts with local people and agencies. Networks were being established and foundations laid for the Basics Bank to grow. Already there were fruitful contacts. A refugee family living in a pitiful situation was helped practically and encouraged spiritually. Their physical situation left their visitor from the Mission "lost for words." The flat was so damp and the conditions so cramped that it was a scene of poverty that Dickens could have been describing in one of his novels. The family with children aged six and eight all shared one room. A typical and often repeated comment from such grateful people was "I don't know how I would have managed without your help."

The Smethams' first full year in charge of the Basics Bank was 2006. They soon won the trust of agencies which referred needy people to the Mission. This was never going to be a 'free for all'

Trevor and Jill Smetham

but a carefully organised work helping genuine cases. Jill and Trevor were determined to treat each referral as an individual. Each person was created by God and special in His sight. This led them to spend quality time with the individuals who called to collect a few basic needs. Within a year the number of referrals had doubled and by the autumn of 2008 the annual figure of individuals seen was heading for 600. One of those precious individuals was a lady from Zimbabwe. She had come to England to study and was being sponsored by a farmer from back home. However when he was driven from his land the money stopped. After months of having no income and living in cramped accommodation she had reached a place of despair. She was put in touch with the Basics Bank and Trevor and Jill gradually won her confidence. It turned out that she had come from a Christian background. Not only did she receive practical help in a time of difficulty but she was encouraged back to faith in Christ.

The expansion of the Basics Bank was again helped by another move of premises. The need for a more permanent home for the Mission had been felt for over a decade. When it became clear in 2005 that the Methodist Church in London Road was to be sold, the Trustees, Missioners and supporters turned to God in prayer. Answers came in several remarkable ways. Calvary Evangelical Church was situated on Viaduct Road behind the fire station in Preston Circus. They had a large first floor room which had been left empty for many years. The Elders and church members at Calvary were excited by the prospect of helping the Mission in this way. Once redeveloped these rooms would provide the Mission with good office facilities for the various projects as well as storage space for the Basics Bank.

However, much work needed to be done to totally refurbish the premises. God answered prayer in this area too. Not only did He provide a Christian architect to advise and oversee the development, but a legacy of over £60,000 came at just the right time to meet all the expenses. The entrance to what became the new Mission Centre, was in Stanley Road, less than a quarter of a mile from the old premises. This made it easy for continuity with the Basic Bank clients to be maintained. This was indeed an encouraging time for the Mission and on May 15th 2006 the whole work was completed and all the projects and administration transferred over to the new premises. The City Mission now had a new centre from which to meet the challenges of the day.

Chapter Fifteen.

Into the Future.

In 2009 the Brighton and Hove City Mission completed 160 years of ministry. In the Autumn of 1849 the prayers and discussions of men like Robert Bevan and Rev. Joseph Sortain had resulted in a seed that was to grow into a missionary work in Brighton and Hove. Hundreds of Christian men and women have faithfully served God through the Mission. Countless thousands have been contacted and given the revolutionary news of the love of God shown through His Son Jesus. If there is still time before the return of Christ we trust that further chapters will be written about the accomplishments of this Mission.

The twin towns have evolved into a City and that 'new city' was seeing enormous changes. Regeneration has altered the face of locations such as the Brighton Station area. Shops, flats and offices now dominate this section of the city. The population continues to grow with the Shoreham-Peacehaven conurbation fast approaching 400,000 people. There are plans to regenerate parts of the sea front and the Marina continues to expand.

Brighton and Hove, like every city, is a dynamic place. Cities are always changing. The one thing that never changes is the Gospel and the need of the human heart. The regeneration that is always required is that of the soul. No one knows what the future holds or what changes in technology will take place. The Mission will always seek to keep up with developments so that the Gospel is shared across the area. The Internet and text messaging are just two new ways in which the Word of God has been made available to the people. One thing is certain. As times change and ideas come and go, the transforming power of the Gospel remains the same.

The Brighton and Hove City Mission steps out into the future looking to God to inspire, shape and provide for this work – His work. Countless saints have helped to make the local City Mission the ministry it has been for 160 years through their service, giving and prayers. If the return of Christ is a long time in coming then we continue to pray that God will be gracious enough to use the efforts of the Brighton and Hove City Mission to speak of His Son, Jesus Christ, and bring glory to His name.

The work continues...until He comes.

Appendix One

BHTM/BHCM Presidents.

No President was appointed until 1877.

The Earl of Chichester 1887-1902
Major-General W C Stileman 1906-1914
Admiral Bernard Currey 1928-1936.
Sir Lancelot Joynson-Hicks MP 1936-1958.
Viscount Brentford 1959-1982.
Rev Canon R J Cobb 1984-1988.
Rev F G Money 1988- 2006

The role has since been discontinued.

Appendix Two

BHTM Vice-Presidents.
(with date of appointment)
This position was introduced in 1929.

Rev C J Gilmore 1929; Rev F Thompson 1929;
Rev Pitt Bonarjee 1929: R A Cripps 1929; Rev T May 1935;
G Oxley 1935; A C Tessier 1935; J H Theakstone 1935;
Rev H J Gregory 1936; J M Waite 1936;
Rev H Tydeman Chilvers1937; Rev E A Chard 1944;
P F Skottowe 1945; G W G Cole 1946; Rev R Rees 1949;
Rev Canon F Ferguson 1951; Rev E Parry Jenkins 1951;
Rev D A Plumley 1951; E G Wade 1953;
Rev W G Oelsner 1958; Rev Canon R J Cobb 1965;
E J Waldron 1976; W L Mills 1983; F G Money 1987.

This role has since been discontinued.

Appendix Three

BHTM /BHCM Chairmen.
(Permanent Chairmen appointed from 1883)

T L Wilson 1883-1885.
Major-General Stileman 1885-1914.
Alexander Townend 1916-1926.
Admiral Bernard Currey 1927-1936.
Horace Richardson 1936-1950.
Rev A Trevor Roberts 1950-1957
A F Carter 1952-1965 (Joint Chairman 1952-1957)
A H Iles 1965-1974.
W L Mills 1974-1977.
R D Pittfield 1978 –1994
R J Wingate 1994-1999
J C Prideaux 1999-

Appendix Four

BHTM/BHCM Secretaries

J Carr 1849-1856 (Joint)
C Eley 1849-1856 (Joint)
Major General Tomkyns 1856-1859 (Joint)
T Warner 1856-1872 (Joint)
T Bigsby Chamberlain 1859-1881 (Joint until 1872)
W Darch 1876-1879 (Joint)
Major General Stileman 1880-1884.
G B Paisley 1883-1891 (Joint)
Major-General Hoste 1885-1891 (Joint)
Rear Admiral R Bingham 1892-1895.
W Hoste 1885-1891 (son of Major General Hoste)
Rev F Thornton Gregg 1897-1898.
Colonel J Phillips 1898-1909
J Haig Waters 1909-1913
Willett Ram 1914-1916
A C Tessier 1916-1923
J H Theakstone 1924-1936
F L Jermym 1936-1941
P F Skottowe 1941-1945
E J Waldron 1945-1971
C Matsell 1971-1977
Rev F G Money 1978-1986
B A Bannier 1986-1993
H W Oakley 1993 –1996 (Business Administrator.)
A W Smith 1996- (Mission Coordinator)

Appendix Five.

BHTM/BHCM Treasurers

T West 1849-1851
R H Madden 1851-1863
T Warner 1863-1872
D Fox 1872-1881
T L Wilson 1881-1882
E H Fosberry 1883-1888
Major-General Wardell 1888-1895
Rear Admiral R Bingham 1895-1923
Vernon Millar 1924-1930
Major R Hamilton 1931-1932
A M Martin 1932-1936
Rev T C Lawson 1937-1941
W Dillistone 1941-1974
B Ward 1974-1977
J Clark 1977-1988
H W Oakley 1989-1996
D Brimley 1996-

Appendix Six

BHCM Council of Reference as on March 1st 2009.

Colin Annis; Sean Avard; Dr John Blanchard;
Chris Butler; Tom Copp; Dr John Etherton;
Rev Derek Fortnum; David Goldin; David Harland;
John Head; Rev Neil Milmine; Rev Philip Moon;
Pastor Stephen Nowak; Harold Oakley; Bob Overton-Hart;
Michael Pope; Andrew Russell; Rev Rhys Stenner;
Steve Walford.

Appendix Seven

BHTM/BHCM Missionaries

E. Anscombe ; L W Adcock; H Baker; B A Bannier;
W Barnes; J Benson; P Bingham; G T Bird; G Bowles;
G Brennan; R S Bridle; D Brimley; V E Burns; T Burros;
W Cadwaller; Mrs J Carroll; G Cooper; P Deuk; A De Souza;
L S Drewett; J Elton; J Flide; D Frost; A Gumbrell;
H G Hacker; C A Hale; G Hall; M Halliday; J B Haynes;
Miss L Hayward; A I Hibberd; A Hughes; D Hughes;
Mrs C Hurd; Miss A G Hurst; A E Jewkes; J J Jones;
W Lamb; T Lawrence; P Malyon; C Manning ; T Martin;
H A Massey; C Matsell; Mrs C Matsell; J McLeod; M McNally;
S Millar; F G Money; G Morgan; G Nind; S Nowak;
Mrs S Nunn; J Pocock; T W Pocock; G Robinson; J Rose;
G W Russell; R H Russell; Mr T & Mrs J Smetham;
A W Smith; W J Sole; F Stevens; Miss M Stone;
G Swanborough; W Taylor; Mrs V Tomsett; E Voke;
E J Waldron; S A Warner; L G Waters; O Wiggett;
H C Wilkins; A Wood.

Appendix Eight.

Schools Workers/ Children's Workers/ Associate Workers.

J Bebb; Mrs L Bolton; Mrs C Boreham; M Edwards;
Miss G Findlay; Mrs L Hall; Miss B Mitchell.

BIBLIOGRAPHY

Information was gleaned from local newspapers such as the Brighton Guardian and from local Directories. Information about the Mission came from the Town Mission Handbooks which date from 1875 and minutes of the Committee meetings. Earlier Handbooks were lost during Mr Chamberlain's time as Secretary. Especially useful was the 'Centenary History of the Brighton and Hove Town Mission' by Rev Pitt Bonarjee.

Briggs A	Victorian Cities	1968
Calder T	The Encyclopaedia of Brighton	1990
Dale A	Fashionable Brighton 1820-1860	1967
Gilbert E W	Brighton Old Ocean's Bauble	1954
Melville L	Brighton: Its History, Its Follies, Its Fashions.	1909
Musgrave C	Life in Brighton	1981
Sala G A	Things I have seen and people I have known	1894
Sala GA	Brighton as I knew it	1898
Underwood E	Brighton	1978